PRAISE FOR *WHAT'S YOUR ENCORE?*

"As an early adopter of coaching people on the nonfinancial aspects of retirement, Larry Jacobson has earned his national recognition as a thought leader in the field. This book's curriculum really does take one from not knowing what to do with one's time in retirement, all the way through to having a plan and knowing the first steps in that plan. Larry goes deep and asks very good questions. The chapters are topics we all face as we turn retirement age, and through the progress you make in the book, Larry helps you redefine the word retirement for your needs and desires. His creativity shines and the writing is five-star all the way. His take on managing your fears is particularly original and his wisdom comes from real experience. This book brings nonfinancial retirement coaching to the masses, and I'm glad to see that it's Larry doing this for all of us."

—**Chip Conley**, founder and CEO of Modern Elder Academy (MEA), author of *Learning to Love Midlife: 12 Reasons Life Gets Better with Age*

"Larry Jacobson is an accomplished and well-respected thought leader in the field of retirement coaching and beyond. In his latest work, *What's Your Encore? A Step-by-Step Guide to Retiring With Purpose and Fulfillment*, Larry provides an engaging experience that helps the reader discover the best of what's next. The exercises have a broad appeal yet remain very personal and meaningful. This is a great addition to your retirement planning library!"

—**Robert Laura**, founder of the Retirement Coaches Association

"Many of us retire and question our 'purpose' in life. We need help, and Larry Jacobson's workbook offers a creative step-by-step approach that will jumpstart new ideas for navigating our retirement years."

—**Sonia Marsh**, author of *Freeways to Flip-Flops* and the *Gutsy Living* blog

"Larry has done it again and the result is a must-read! Combine corporate expertise, decades of experience, wisdom, a six-year sailing adventure around the globe, and practical application coaching clients from broad industries/all walks of life, and the result...a book destined to be an important go-to guide. Larry has always promoted having a purpose and a plan. This book shows you how. Don't retire without it."

—**Joyce Cohen**, career transition and life planning specialist, cofounder of My Future Purpose, author of Diving Into Living...My Way series

"Larry Jacobson's *What's Your Encore?* is an essential guide for anyone standing at the precipice of retirement. Meticulously crafted, it offers a unique blend of insightful exercises, practical strategies, and heartfelt advice, ensuring your retirement journey is not just planned, but purposeful and fulfilling. Jacobson's expertise shines through every page, transforming the daunting task of retirement planning into an inspiring voyage of self-discovery and passion pursuit. A must-read for those seeking a vibrant and meaningful post-career life."

—**Patricia Fripp**, CSP, CPAE, former president of the National Speakers Association, author of *Deliver Unforgettable Presentations*

"*What's Your Encore?* by Larry Jacobson is a rare must-read in the crowded field of life fulfillment books. Larry powerfully guides you to make the most of your long future with clarity and purpose. Enjoy all the elements of the perfect how-to book coupled with deep emotional intelligence, as you create new possibilities for yourself that are practical, inspirational, and resultful. Larry shows you how to find your passion, prioritize your actions, and realize your retirement dreams. This is not a read-it-and-forget-it book. You will revisit its wisdom repeatedly throughout the fabulous decades ahead."

—**Adriane Berg**, founder of Generation Bold Consulting, author of *How Not To Go Broke at 102* and *The Totally Awesome Money Book for Kids,* Emmy Award-winning host of *Tax Beat*, and United Nations representative at the International Federation on Ageing

"I just turned seventy-eight, and I'm tired. Should I retire? I'm in pretty good health, and I could use the money from continuing to work. Should I move to assisted living? Do I really *need* to? Shouldn't I move in *before* I need to? Or should I?

The questions were endless, each opening yet another question. These were the sorts of things I would formerly chew over with my husband. They were plaguing me, and my husband was no longer available.

I turned to Larry Jacobson, retirement coach. He listened carefully and inquired about the countless and very particular factors of my unique life situation. Being a rabbi, I am aware that each person's case is unlike any other and needs its own wise consideration. At the conclusion of his guidance, I felt clear and confident in what my next moves should be.

I am delighted to see that this book is available to help so many of us who are aging. This last phase of life is one that our culture is not so eager to embrace, consequently leaving many of us without the guidance we need. But here it is! This book will companion you with assurance as you step into your new self, maximizing your opportunities for joy and fulfillment."

—**Rabbi Me'irah Iliinsky**, MSW, MA Hebrew Letters, community rabbi at Rhoda Goldman Plaza Assisted Living Center, author of *Mapping the Journey: The Mourner & the Soul*, director of the School of Jewish Living Arts

"Larry has written the book that will take you from wondering what's next to developing a vision and goals for an inspiring life beyond retirement. He has lived this type of transition and shares his wisdom, thoughts, and helpful exercises throughout. My clients speak about their fear of being bored. They feel unmoored and unmotivated. I look forward to sharing *What's Your Encore?* with them."

—**Wendy Green**, life coach and podcast host of *Hey, Boomer!*

"Did you know that the Baby Boomer generation is turning retirement upside down? They're starting new careers, pursuing new hobbies, finding passions, and discovering that life has so much more.

Retirement is *yours* to create. It's no longer an endgame, but instead, it can be an incredible beginning for you of discovery, joy, and passion!

Ask yourself: *What's on my bucket list? What things in life do I still want to achieve? How can I create new beginnings? Are there things I want to do, but something is holding me back? How can I start living a new revitalized version of my life? Is* this *all there is?*

If you didn't quickly answer the above to your satisfaction, then this book is for you. You'll find how you can define retirement *by your own rules*. Larry will help guide you to discover a whole new gear to your life, *and* you will discover that your retirement years can be the greatest chapter yet!"

—**Suzanne Perkins Newman**, founder of 12 Days to Goodness, and founder and chief executive officer of Answers for Elders, Inc.

"Every retiree struggles somewhat with the loss of identity and social network from their careers. Many are unsure of what to do with themselves each day after their career ends. Many mistake pleasure with fulfillment. Not only does Larry explain all of these ideas with great clarity, he guides the reader to choose a direction. He helps you find your true passion, helps you combine that with your skills from work, and guides you to determine what it is you want to do with the rest of your life. His stories come to life and pop right off the page, giving you real life examples of his work in action. And Larry's experiences are what gives him the wisdom to help the rest of us find our way."

—**Keith Schaefer**, cofounder and managing partner of Zermatt Capital Partners

"Very few people in the US know retirement like Larry Jacobson. He has been there and done it and now has a proven method for helping others make the hard decisions about how they want to live and what they want to do in their later years. Larry proved himself to be an inspiring writer in *The Boy Behind the Gate,* and with *What's Your Encore?*, he demonstrates yet again how much he has to share with fellow retirees *or* un-retirees. Larry accomplishes this with loads of worksheets, checklists, a mountain of useful information."

—**Sara Zeff Geber**, PhD, professional speaker and author of *Essential Retirement Planning for Solo Agers*

"I recommend Larry Jacobson's new workbook, *What's Your Encore?: A Step-by-Step Guide to Retiring with Purpose and Fulfillment.* It's filled with great information, resources, and exercises! Larry fulfilled his dream to sail around the world. Since then he has combined his life experiences with his business and coaching expertise to help others realize their own dreams. He initially chronicled his own experiences and discoveries in his wonderful book, *The Boy Behind the Gate.* Then, wanting to reach more people, he developed his award-winning video training course, Sail into Retirement. Influenced by this online course, this new workbook will inspire and challenge you to create your own retirement journey. It's fun, upbeat, and inspiring! Using sailing metaphors, he helps us chart our own course and offers tools as well as an action guide to help us navigate our own challenging transition and to create our best possible life!"

—**Dorian Mintzer**, MSW, PhD, BCC, therapist, speaker, owner and host of the *Revolutionize your Retirement Interview with Experts* podcast series and monthly program, and co-author of *The Couple's Retirement Puzzle: 10 Must-Have Conversations for Creating an Amazing New Life Together*

"Working with Larry as a coach has been immensely valuable as I navigate multiple transitions in my life, especially retirement. Larry's excellent listening abilities and forward thinking have helped me discover and discern what really matters to me. His knowledge, experience, and wisdom have helped immensely in how to work with the challenges and opportunities I am confronted with as I age. Now that he has put all of this into his new book, *What's Your Encore?*, many more people will have access to his coaching, and that can only be a good thing! Larry is a joy to work with; an ally, a coach, and an inspiration all rolled into one. I consider crossing paths with Larry to be one of my life's great blessings. His book is a must-read."

—**Captain Jan Passion**, executive coach

"Do you often find yourself daydreaming about a path yet unexplored? Life often poses challenging questions that prompt us to reassess our journey. These inquiries can spark thoughtful reflection and a yearning to venture into uncharted territory. Amidst our hectic routines, we seldom pause to ponder, *What's next for me?* Let Larry Jacobson guide you on a journey of self-discovery through his latest book, *What's Your Encore? A Step-by-Step Guide to Retiring With Purpose and Fulfillment*. What sets Jacobson apart is his ability not only to lead and inspire your exploration, but also to intimately share his own adventures with a delightful blend of humor and wisdom. Allow him to be your companion in uncovering the next chapter of your life."

—**Luanne Mullin**, transition coach and facilitator, director and managing partner of Luanne Mullin Partnerships

"As a psychiatrist, patients often say to me, 'I just want to be happy.' In response, I ask, 'How will you know when you get there?' For many, work has defined them, and they have never visualized a life beyond the end of their career. *What's Your Encore?* by Larry Jacobson leads retirees step by step to dream of a retirement of purpose and meaning and how to achieve it. That's what will make them happy in their new life."

—**Loren A. Olson**, MD, psychiatrist, author of the award-winning book, *No More Neckties: A Memoir in Essays*

"I have known and worked with Larry Jacobson for many years and he is an inspiring teacher and writer. This well-written and timely book is a much-needed roadmap for Baby Boomers as they enter retirement. Based on his life experience this book will show you how to find your passion and pursue it! Every retiree will find this illuminating."

—**Mitch Meyerson**, co-author of eleven books and four online programs, including *Guerilla Marketing*

"Joseph Campbell made famous the phrase 'follow your bliss.' Larry Jacobson has taken this proclamation to the next level for those entering the retirement zone of their life. His new book, *What's Your Encore? A Step-by-Step Guide to Retiring With Purpose and Fulfillment,* is a personalized, creative roadmap to transcend your former life and enter your retirement phase with a vision, a gameplan, and a transformational new identity.

I've known Larry for over thirty years. I watched him soar as an entrepreneurial CEO, only to sell his company and pursue his retirement dream of sailing around the world. And, as in "The Hero's Journey," he returned to our world, bringing his experiences and sagacious advice for others seeking a new kind of fulfillment and bliss in their own retirement.

What makes Larry brilliant is his *experiential wisdom*. A practitioner of ancient and modern philosophies, he brings emotional empathy to new retirees with ingenious insights and inspiring advice from his 'been there, done that' point of view. With Larry's game plan, retirement is not to be feared, but celebrated with 'the best is yet to come.' "

—**Jim Spencer Hall**, president of The Creative Circle, Inc.

"Larry has been our go-to public speaking coach for the Young Entrepreneur Success YES! Accelerator. He is a nurturing pitch coach who provides not only experience in the entrepreneurial world, but also a toolkit that the young entrepreneurs can easily follow for a successful three-minute pitch. We appreciate the passion Larry brings to our community of mentors, and we are delighted to see him conquer a new summit with this book."

—**Amparo Leyman Pino**, MEd, director of education at BizWorld.org, Fulbright Specialist, and author of *Breaking the Silos: Science Communication for Everyone*

"As a physician, I have treated many patients who retired. Soon after retiring, unsurprisingly, many sustain a cardiovascular event, whether it be a heart attack or stroke. Whether it be the sudden lack of stimulation, loss of self-esteem, boredom, etc., it is a sudden change. This abrupt change in emotional dynamics has a potential harmful effect on physical dynamics. This is why I have found this book by the experienced life coach Larry Jacobson to be intriguing and potentially life-saving for many. There are some simple questions which stimulate you to think. The in-book workshops are helpful in focusing and creating direction. Overall the workbook serves as an excellent guide to a meaningful life into retirement."

—**E. Mike Vasilomanolakis**, MD, cardiologist, assistant clinical professor at the University of California Irvine, executive producer of Grammy-winning New Age album *Echoes of Love,* and author of *Lists for a Great Life*

"Larry Jacobson has integrated a boatload of wisdom, spiced with his unique life experience, into a valuable retirement planner that provides both practical and inspiring steps to planning your retirement years. This book can take the place of a retirement coach—if you commit to engaging in the process of self-assessment and follow-up actions, always leaving room for unexpected opportunities."

—**Meg L. Newhouse**, PhD, author of *Legacies of the Heart: Living a Life That Matters*, and creator of www.passionandpurpose.com

"Larry writes about one of my favorite themes: how to be sure you have a sense of purpose in your life when you "retire." If you want to take charge of your own destiny, and not just react to what life throws you in retirement, the process and exercises in this workbook are invaluable."

—**Richard Caro**, cofounder of Tech-enhanced Life, PBC

"Hope all those contemplating retirement years will gift themselves this workbook to craft a compelling, exciting, and vivid image for a meaningful and fulfilling future. Using engaging questions and a step-by-step guide, you're invited to take a deep dive to discover your passions and to create a clear path to bring your vision to life."

—**Barbara Abramowitz**, psychotherapist, body-mind life coach, and contributor to *Live Smart After 50!*

"For those who wish to ensure that their retirement will be a success, I cannot recommend Jacobson's *What's Your Encore?* enough. Using his own considerable experience, Larry walks the reader through the mental and physical steps necessary to retire with a sense of purpose and contentment.

It is significant that Larry does not skip the mental exercises that enable one to envision the life of possibilities that await. Too few people take the preemptive steps warranted by such a big life event as retirement. We plan our careers, we plan our weddings, we plan our vacations, but that last big event in your life will be your retirement. Why not plan your final years out so that you are assured a happy and fulfilling final chapter? Filled with joy and humor, *What's Your Encore?* will enable you to approach retirement with enthusiasm and confidence. As you read and complete the exercises, expect to get excited by all that is possible for you in the near future."

—**Rumana Jabeen**, MA Sociology, realtor and KW Real Estate Planner

"I was the classic prospective candidate for Larry's teachings. Recently retired with no plan as to what my real vision of the future looked like. Larry's program opened my eyes to how to write that workbook of my retirement goals. He employs the same principles I used in my business days such as SWOT analysis, Decision-Making, and Managing Your Fears, and does it in an intuitive, insightful way. Every retiree should read this book, it's never too early to start preparing for the next chapter of your life!"

—**David Cullen**, CEO of JP Cullen, coaching client and pupil of Larry's Sail into Retirement program

"When I first encountered Larry's teachings during a module for my Retirement Management Advisor designation course, I had no idea the impact it would have on my perspective. Larry's insights delved into a crucial yet often overlooked aspect of retirement: the loss of identity, purpose, and loved ones that can profoundly affect one's happiness and well-being.

Larry's expertise resonated with me so deeply that I immediately implemented his strategies in my client planning. I also extended an invitation for him to share his wisdom on my podcast, recognizing the invaluable contribution he could make to my audience.

What Larry imparts goes beyond the financial strategies advisors tend to focus on with their clients; it's about understanding the intricate nuances of a fulfilling retirement—one that encompasses joy, peace of mind, and overall health. Through his course, I've gained a deeper understanding of how to serve my clients better, equipping me with the tools to navigate not just their financial needs, but their emotional and psychological well-being as well.

Larry's book is a must-read for anyone embarking on or navigating retirement. It encapsulates the essence of his teachings, offering invaluable insights that can truly transform one's perspective on what it means to retire happily and meaningfully. I wholeheartedly endorse Larry's work and am grateful for the profound impact it has had on my practice and the lives of those I serve."

—**John Iammarino**, RMA, president of Securus Financial, co-host of *The Retire Happy Podcast*

"Thanks to Larry, I was able make a successful transition from a corporate insurance leader to a self-employed advisor and coach. I learned about Larry on my sixtieth birthday. He was participating in a webinar, and I was trying to figure out how to get out of the corporate rat race and finally be fulfilled and happy. Larry demonstrated an amazing depth of understanding nonfinancial retirement issues. That webinar was the beginning of a new and better life. Working though my hopes and fears with Larry's step-by-step approach gave me the courage to make a change.

In *What's Your Encore?,* Larry takes you step by step through the process of a successful retirement. Do you want more from your life? If so, using Larry's proven approach to retirement success will change your life! Buy this book and live the life that you've always dreamed of!"

—**Mike Rozema**, founder and CEO of Actuarial Excellence LLC, coaching client and pupil of Larry's Sail into Retirement program

"I have known Larry Jacobson for over fifty years, read with great interest his book *The Boy Behind the Gate* about his adventures sailing around the world, and have seen and read his advice for seniors on navigating retirement and aging. His writing and speaking style is accessible and entertaining and imbued with wisdom, positive energy, and advice. They reflect his personal qualities of intelligence, empathy, warmth, and caring. All of this is reflected in *What's Your Encore?* in which Larry helps make aging an adventure, a pleasurable experience, and a purposeful next stage of life."

—**G.W. McDonald**, retired enforcement attorney of the California Department of Corporations

"As someone who believes it's never too late to find your true calling, the way Larry has reinvented himself to help others find their post-career passion reminds me once again of the courage it takes to be all of who we are. This book will help anybody find their true self. Larry is inspiring, a good writer, and the book is truly practical."

—**Jane Fleishman**, PhD, MEd, sexuality educator, author of *The Stonewall Generation: LGBTQ Elders on Sex, Aging, and Activism*, winner of the 2020 Nautilus Award

"Where most retirement planning books focus on financial security, Larry anchors retirement planning around the human in the middle of it. His roadmap is not a slog of financial planning, it's an exciting exploration into what we value and the stories and adventures about our own lives that are yet untold. I've been privileged to work with Larry. His own inspirational story will no doubt inspire anyone who follows his path."

—**Tina Mulqueen**, international speaker, writer, founder of Kindred PR, adjunct professor at WSU, and two-time Top 100 Women in Media

WHAT'S YOUR ENCORE?

BOOKS BY LARRY JACOBSON

The Boy Behind the Gate: How His Dream of Sailing Around the World Became a Six-Year Odyssey of Adventure, Fear, Discovery, and Love

The Retirement Challenge: A Non-Financial Guide from Top Retirement Experts

Navigating Entrepreneurship: 11 Proven Keys to Success

Let's Go!: The Adventures of Skip and Kanek

WHAT'S YOUR ENCORE?

A Step-by-Step Guide to Retiring

With Purpose and Fulfillment

LARRY JACOBSON

Copyright © 2024 by Larry Jacobson.
Published by Buoy Press, Emeryville, California

Cover Design: Elina Diaz
Cover Photo/illustration: stock.adobe.com/Maria, stock.adobe.com/dumayne
Interior illustrations and photos: Larry Jacobson
Layout & Design: Elina Diaz

Uploading or distributing photos, scans or any content from this book without prior permission is theft of the author's intellectual property. Please honor the author's work as you would your own. Thank you in advance for respecting our author's rights.

For permission requests, please contact the publisher at:
Buoy Press
Emeryville, California
info@BuoyPress.com

For special orders, quantity sales, course adoptions, and corporate sales, trade, and wholesale sales, please contact the publisher at the same email address above.

What's Your Encore? A Step-by-Step Guide to Retiring with Purpose and Fulfillment

ISBN: 978-0-9828787-3-6

This book is dedicated to all of the smart people who admit when they don't know something. You have the courage to stand up and say, "I don't know," and you are smart enough to ask for help from someone who does. You will go far.

"If you don't know where you are going,
how will you know when you get there?"

—Larry Jacobson

TABLE OF CONTENTS

FOREWORD	21
PREFACE **Do You Have a Plan?**	23
WHY SHOULD YOU LISTEN TO LARRY?	25
CHAPTER ZERO **So Many Questions**	29
CHAPTER 1 **Visioning Your Dream**	35
CHAPTER 2 **Turning Your Dreams into Goals**	64
CHAPTER 3 **Your Personal SWOT Analysis**	76
CHAPTER 4 **Elements of a Balanced Lifestyle**	86
CHAPTER 5 **Risk Analysis**	112
CHAPTER 6 **Personal Decision-Making**	122
CHAPTER 7 **Managing Your Fears**	130
CHAPTER 8 **Finding and Keeping a Positive Perspective**	142
CHAPTER 9 **Perseverance—Sticking with It**	149
CHAPTER 10 **Commitment to Your Plan of Action**	158
CHAPTER 11 **Your Encore Plan**	173
BONUS CHAPTER 12 **Begin with the End**	183
AFTERWORD	189
ACKNOWLEDGEMENTS	191
ABOUT THE AUTHOR	192

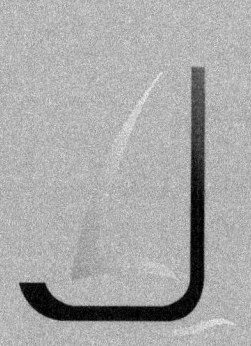

FOREWORD

Of all the people I've met as a public official over the past fourteen years, Larry Jacobson is one of the most fascinating. I had the privilege of meeting Larry—or Captain Larry—in 2015 when he captained a boat on the San Francisco Bay for me and my friends to watch the Navy's Blue Angels fly during Fleet Week. We've remained friends since. I was honored when he reached out to me and asked me to write the foreword for his workbook.

I have watched family and colleagues struggle with the "what next?" of retirement after hustling their way to the top of their fields. That's why I know this workbook will help be a vessel of hope for future retirees. Retirement is not the end of the road, but rather the beginning of a new open highway. Or as Larry would say, "uncharted waters!" The possibilities don't stop, so neither should you.

It can be easy for our careers to become our identities. I'm confident that with the help of this workbook, you can take the first steps to planning a retirement that will open new doors and discover new passions.

No matter the age, life will always throw us curveballs. That is why it is up to us to embrace change and not run from it. Your ideal retirement is decided on your terms and on your time.

Take this opportunity for what it is: a new chapter. One where you can write the rules and enjoy all the benefits.

—**Eric Swalwell**, congressman, California 14th District, author of *Endgame*

PREFACE

DO YOU HAVE A PLAN?

When I ask people what they are going to do upon retiring, the most common answer I hear is, "I'm going to sleep late, travel, and write my memoir." When I ask where they will get their purpose and fulfillment, I am often met with silence. It's not something most people think about until they're facing a whole lot of time on their hands and uncertainty how to fill that time in a meaningful way. Whether you are considering retirement fairly soon, have just retired, or have been retired for a while, you must be asking yourself, *What am I going to do next?* What will you do with your time all day?

Most likely, you have a financial plan for retirement, but two out of three of you do not have a non-fiscal plan. Maybe you have enough money to retire, or perhaps you still need additional income. Either way, you are still faced with the question of: *How will I spend my days...and my years*? Without a route to follow, it's easy to drift aimlessly.

This book is about transition, and it is designed intentionally to help you create a retirement of purpose and fulfillment. *What's Your Encore?* cracks the code to helping you create the best possible life for your golden years. The methods, tools, lessons, and Action Guide are based on my proven award-winning coaching program, *Sail Into Retirement.* It is specifically designed to help you find, develop, and follow your passion while living a balanced life. Your encore will come from combining that passion with your skills, expertise, experience, knowledge, and wisdom from your career and personal life.

From my coaching experience, I see most people spend more time planning their next car purchase than what to do with their time in retirement. This book will help you take an active and focused role in designing your own time and transforming the quality of your life for now and the future.

What's Your Encore? is fun, upbeat, and inspiring. Upon completing the book and exercises, you'll feel good about where you're going with your future and the life of your dreams. Simply follow the step-by-step directions, as each provides you with exercises that build on each other. You'll end up with a plan to transform your retirement into one you'll absolutely be passionate about, one that will make you jump out of bed with joy and anticipation of another great day to be alive.

—Larry Jacobson

WHY SHOULD YOU LISTEN TO LARRY?

The author, Larry Jacobson.

Why Larry? What makes him *the expert* in the field? The answer is simple: Because he developed the lessons in this book based on his own experience searching for purpose and fulfillment, and his discovery of satisfaction in the work of helping others find their purpose and fulfillment. He is a trusted national authority on non-fiscal retirement planning. Larry believes only in teaching what he knows, and turning your passion into your dream retirement is a field he knows very well. He is a regular speaker on retirement lifestyle planning related topics at corporate training events, conferences, retreats, and he has twice been invited to present his story on the TEDx stage.

Larry was recently awarded the coveted award of "Retirement Catalyst Coach of the Year." He's the real deal. Indeed, Jacobson's story is one we have all wanted to live. At the age of thirteen, Jacobson taught himself to sail in a tiny boat on Alamitos Bay, in Long Beach. From that day forward, he dreamed of sailing around the world as captain of his own cruising sailboat.

Larry Jacobson at age sixteen in Long Beach.

And then life happened. He grew up and entered the corporate world, but never lost the passion for his dream. After twenty years in business as a vice-president, president, and CEO, he decided that was enough. He exited the corporate world, and thirty-three years after first stepping foot in that tiny sailboat, Jacobson sailed out the Golden Gate on a six-year journey around the world. He followed his passion and made his dream come true.

Larry's return from his six-year circumnavigation.

Loss of identity is the most difficult issue for most new retirees. "The hardest part was letting go of my identity," says Jacobson, "who I was, who I had created myself to be during a twenty-year business career. While working, I felt valued, important, and that I was contributing. Leaving that all behind was a most difficult decision."

Yet, while searching for happiness in the distant corners of the globe, he realized it wasn't only achieving his dream that gave him satisfaction. The true feeling of growth, reward, and self-actualization came from inspiring others to achieve their dreams.

After writing the award-winning memoir about his six-year journey, *The Boy Behind the Gate*, Jacobson began sharing his motivational message through speaking and coaching. Today, his motivation and satisfaction come from helping you to find your passion, plan an amazing retirement, and achieve your dreams.

"How did you do it? How did you get through the fears, the decision-making, the risks, and the process of letting go of your former career identity?" These are the questions Jacobson is asked most frequently. In response to countless people wanting answers, Jacobson went to work. He spent a year reverse engineering the process he'd experienced, analyzing every step of the way from leaving his career to sailing out the Golden Gate. He knows the questions to ask and in what order to ask them, and he knows how to get results—because he has actually done it.

What makes this book unique? *What's Your Encore?* is based on experience rather than theory. The value is in the results. It comes not only from the information, but also the system Jacobson uses in the book and personal coaching sessions. The lessons build on one another in a logical order, ensuring the best results. From his graduate work in education at the University of California at Berkeley, Jacobson understands sequencing of learning and building a platform of knowledge step by step. He has developed this system with your success in mind, and you will complete the book with a plan in hand.

—E.G. Sebastian, life coach to Larry Jacobson

CHAPTER ZERO
SO MANY QUESTIONS

Welcome to *What's Your Encore? A Step-by-Step Guide to Retiring With Purpose and Fulfillment*. In this book, we'll take an unconventional look at retirement, navigating through a series of lessons to chart the course to the retirement of your dreams. Retirement "success" depends on using your passion, alongside your skills, expertise, talent, knowledge, and experience, to live your life as you want. It may happen in phases.

You may not go from what you're currently doing to suddenly leaving the dock to sail across an ocean because *transitions are a process, not an event*. Your big dream can come at once or in steps. You may even decide to pursue multiple dreams and go through this process several times as you move from one episode to another. Regardless of how you move forward with the transition process, what you read here will apply. In fact, it will apply to any transition you might be experiencing.

But first, here are some things you'll need to know as we work through these lessons. This book is comprised of twelve chapters plus various interactive exercises in the Action Guide. Notice that some chapters have multiple parts to them. Every chapter contains an Action Guide, usually at the end of the chapter, which will help you plan each step toward a retirement of purpose, fulfillment, and joy. Consider the Action Guide to be the navigational tool you can refer back to any time you need a little motivation to stay on course. Take care to complete it thoughtfully and thoroughly so that by the end of this book, you'll have mapped out your journey. The Action Guide will become your plan to get you started and keep you on course. If you have questions or comments or need additional support in any of the chapters, please reach out to me via www.LarryJacobson.com/contact.

This book is filled with questions, some of which are difficult to answer and call for deep thinking. And while some questions may seem difficult, don't despair—this process is supposed to be fun. Please trust the system and answer the questions as best you can, but don't get stuck on any of them. If you don't have an answer, move on and come back to it later.

We're going to jump right in with both feet, and your first step is to answer questions in your Action Guide. Your answers to the questions may be as broad or specific as you like. Don't be afraid to think big. Don't overthink your answers. Go with your first gut reaction since there is no rule against changing your answers later if you wish.

ACTION GUIDE 1: DEEP THINKING

As mentioned, the Action Guide is most often found at the end of chapters. However, there are some questions scattered throughout the book, like those below, that should be answered when you first see them. You'll be glad you did because they are designed to keep your creative juices flowing. I'll ask you these same questions again at the end of the book, and comparing your answers in both places is a fun and revealing exercise. If you are unsure of the answers to any questions, skip them, making a note to come back to them at a later time. For now, we want to identify any preconceptions you have about your retirement lifestyle, so go ahead and write down the answers to the questions below. They may require some deep thinking. Can you write in the book? Of course you can, it's yours!

1. What is it that you really want in life?

   _____

   _____

   _____

   _____

   _____

2. What makes you really happy or gives you satisfaction?

   _____

   _____

   _____

   _____

   _____

3. What cause, passion, or purpose keeps you going when times get tough?

_____

_____

_____

_____

_____

4. When you're on your last breath, what will you be glad you did?

_____

_____

_____

_____

_____

5. When you're on your last breath, what will you wish you had done?

_____

_____

_____

_____

_____

6. What do you want to create?

_____

_____

_____

_____

_____

7. What do you want to contribute?

_____

_____

_____

_____

_____

8. What do you want people to say about you after you're gone?

_____

_____

_____

_____

_____

9. How do you want the world to see you as a person?

_____

_____

_____

_____

_____

10. When will you take your first step in pursuing your retirement ambitions?

_____

_____

_____

_____

_____

CHAPTER 1

VISIONING YOUR DREAM

I dreamt the same dream for thirty years. When I closed my eyes, I saw myself standing behind the wheel of my own sailboat gliding out the Golden Gate. If I kept my eyes closed, I saw myself sitting on a white sand beach under a swaying palm tree in front of a turquoise blue bay, feeling the warm tropical trade winds on my skin. And if I kept my eyes closed long enough and kept the vision in my mind, I could see myself sailing back underneath the Golden Gate Bridge after sailing around the world. My vision was so clear: I could see friends and family standing on the bridge cheering. I could see boats coming out to greet us; I could see dozens of people standing on the dock; and I could hear popping champagne corks flying. And guess what? That is exactly the way it happened. After six years, forty thousand nautical miles, and forty countries, we sailed back under the Gate.

What's your dream? What's your vision? This book is about making your vision a reality, but first we have to know in detail what it looks like. Don't have a vision yet? We'll discover your vision together. This is about taking you to the next step in life so you can achieve true fulfillment through self-actualization.

Remember Maslow and his hierarchy of needs? You probably studied it in Psychology 101. You've likely already mastered the first four levels of the hierarchy, all the way through self-esteem.

Maslow's hierarchy of needs by Abraham Maslow

However, you're here reading this book because something is missing in your life: self-actualization. It's not uncommon to go through life and never achieve self-actualization. But being here reading this book is a good first step to achieving the top of the pyramid.

If you haven't already identified your big dream, that's what this chapter is about—identifying your dream. If you already have a dream and know what your next step is, then you will use this exercise to fill in the details of what you see in that dream. Through introspection and a passion quiz, you're going to identify and envision your big dream. By the end of this chapter, you'll have made your dream tangible by writing it down—and that's a big step.

Let's begin by asking more questions of yourself. I suggest you answer the following questions below so you can refer to them later on in the book. Skip any questions you like, but make a note to come back to them at a later time.

1. Ask yourself what have you done in the past that made you happy?

_____

_____

_____

_____

_____

_____

_____

_____

2. What have you done that didn't make you happy?

_____

_____

_____

_____

_____

_____

_____

_____

3. Are you driven by purpose?

　

4. What are your intentions?

5. What will make you jump out of bed in the morning?

_____

_____

_____

_____

_____

_____

_____

_____

6. What do you daydream about? What images do you see in your head when you think about your future?

_____

_____

_____

_____

_____

_____

_____

If you can't be very specific, imagine what it would be like to be so dedicated and passionate about something that you couldn't wait for each day's sunrise. See yourself wanting to get out of bed to do something…of your choosing. While you're doing this, notice if little pictures start popping into your head. Those pictures are clues to your desires and passions.

Many professionals find they're very good at business, but fear moving on to philanthropy, travel, adventure, writing, art, speaking, and mentorship because it's out of their comfort zone. Ask yourself how comfortable you are helping entrepreneurs, teaching business to kids, teaching ethics in business, joining Doctors Without Borders, helping kids learn to read, or building on or repairing the mark you and your company have left on the world? How about creating a new product or service? Becoming an author or an artist?

If you are one of the many who just doesn't know what to do for an encore, please don't fret about it—it's not your fault. Why don't most of you have a plan?

- You didn't know you were going to live so long. Baby Boomers are living twenty to thirty years longer than previous generations. This is new. Baby Boomers are the first generation to be given a blank scene in your life script that has never existed before. What an opportunity!

- You were never told you were going to need a plan, and therefore don't know how to write one. You have been following a script for most of your life. When unsure of your lines or what to do next, you could simply look at the script.

- You were never taught how to make a plan for retirement.

- Creating your plan takes some thinking, visioning, asking yourself lots of questions—*and answering them.*

Picture the script from a play and how it flows from scene to scene. Does any of this script sound familiar when it comes to your life?

You went to kindergarten through elementary school, then junior high school, then high school. Without much ado, you followed the script through high school and graduated. With little time to breathe, you likely then went to college, university, military or police academy, medical school, or a tech or trade school.

If you went into the restaurant industry, the promotions may have followed a script of climbing a ladder: prep cook, line cook, hot side, sous chef, and finally executive chef/restaurant owner. If you were in the military, your time in the service took you from private on up the ladder, and maybe you even made it to the rank of general.

Entrepreneurs and business owners also may follow a script: Build your business, play tennis on Saturdays, find your exit strategy, and get out. Get out to what?

> If you are going to retire *from* something, then you should also be retiring *to* something.

For most of you, the screenplay ends here. You made it as far as you could or wanted to. Now, eager for the next thing and ready for your encore, you turn the page, and there's nothing on it. It's a total blank. And as they say on Broadway, "If it ain't on the page, it ain't on the stage." So we'd better write that script.

"What are my lines? What should I do?" The play of life keeps going, but you no longer have a part in the play. In order to write your script and get back into the play, you need to do some deep thinking. Remember, you get to do what you want—and this presents a problem. This is where I often hear clients say, "But I don't know what I want to do." For most people, finding the answer is a daunting task. But isn't it funny how after following plans for much of our lives, when we're finally given the chance to write our own script, most of us don't do it. I have clients who are CEOs and who've written multiple business plans but don't have a nonfinancial retirement plan for themselves. Where do you start? Right here. We're going to create a vision in your head, and please keep the following in mind about how our brains work.

USE YOUR EMOTIONS

When you envision your big dream, forget your current circumstances. Set your sights on what you want, not what you think you can have. This is thinking with the right side of your brain: the emotional side, not the logical side. Be illogical; it's okay for what you see to be dreamy and imaginative.

USE YOUR LOGIC

When you envision your big dream, it's important not only to see the big picture, but to paint in the details, which come from the left side of your brain. So, when visioning, it's important to combine both sides and use all of your senses. For example, when I dreamed of sailing around the world, I could:

- See the turquoise water
- Feel the sand between my toes
- See the swaying palm trees
- Smell and taste the salt air
- Hear the wind rushing through the palm trees

In other visions, I could see my boat alone out in the middle of an ocean, and I could also see myself at the wheel. I could identify so many details in my mind that I was almost able to make myself seasick from the big ocean swells!

What about your vision? When you imagine your dream future, what is it that you see, hear, smell, taste, and feel? Describe your vision of your ideal retirement future in as much sensory detail as possible here:

PROPER ANCHORING IS NOT JUST FOR BOATS, IT'S FOR YOUR LIFE

What are the anchors that are your foundation supporting your intentions? Let me explain. Sailing around the world teaches you to have faith in your anchor. Sometimes it was nerve-wracking waiting to see whether or not the anchor would hold, but after learning proper techniques, we knew we could trust the anchor to hold us through the worst of conditions. That's a physical anchor.

Then there are emotional anchors, and they keep you grounded (pun intended). Your personal life anchors are mental convictions you can always count on to guide you and keep you on course. My anchors keep me centered; not 100 percent of the time, but they usually keep me from drifting too far. By sharing my life anchors, I hope to inspire you to establish your own personal anchors. Here is what I have posted on my bathroom mirror:

1. I can direct my life by the actions I take. I choose where to set the anchor. If I don't like where I am anchored, I should move.

2. I establish my own values and morals.

3. I continually refine my goals and visions. I want them manageable, achievable, and far-reaching.

4. I always strive to improve in character and craft.

5. I appreciate those around me and strive to let them know.

6. I enjoy the view and mark the worth of every day.

YOUR ANCHORS

Take a few moments to identify your anchors by reflecting on your values, morals, and emotional convictions. If you are unsure of your anchors, come back to this section when you have more clarity on them. Or you can just write one for now.

1. What are some values or moral convictions that guide your life?

   _____

   _____

   _____

2. Which of the above supports you in your journey toward your encore?

   _____

   _____

   _____

3. Which of the above anchors hold you back from realizing your major life-changing goals?

   _____

   _____

   _____

4. How do you want to incorporate your positive anchors into your retirement?

_____
_____
_____
_____
_____
_____
_____
_____
_____

I have heard, "I have all of this business experience, but I really just want to paint." Then why not paint? Perhaps due to guilt that you're not using your talents to their full potential? Paint. And then start a school for underprivileged kids to learn to paint. Or organize and lead mural painting in the inner city.

Is it logical? Does it matter? (My sailing journey was illogical, but I went anyway.) Why not let your heart and emotional desire lead for a change? This is difficult, I know. I have been there and have been through the same thinking process, and I recognize it's not that easy to let go, dream, and imagine.

> In our careers, we are used to having all of our ducks in a row, and now I'm asking you to let the ducks sit wherever they want.

THE PASSION QUIZ

In addition to the questions you answered at the beginning of the book, there are just a few more. Before we create a vision statement, let's identify or reinforce your passion with the Passion Quiz. When you go through these questions, try to answer them fairly quickly. Don't ponder any one question too long as we are looking for the first things that come into your mind. Don't be afraid of duplicate answers, we are looking for patterns and duplicates.

1. What makes you smile?

   _____

   _____

   _____

2. What makes you leap out of bed in the morning (without coffee)?

   _____

   _____

   _____

3. We all find ourselves in moments when we feel most alive—almost invincible. What activity or activities make you feel like that?

   _____

   _____

   _____

   _____

4. What do people thank you for most often?

_____

_____

_____

_____

_____

5. On what subject(s) do people (often) ask you for advice?

_____

_____

_____

_____

_____

6. What are you really good at doing? What are your precious gifts? Include the gifts or strengths that come naturally to you—some of which you might even take for granted (including skills, knowledge of a specific topic, great public speaking abilities, great listener, etc.)

_____

_____

_____

_____

7. Who do you look up to? Who do you see as your mentors? Who inspires you? Why?

_____

_____

_____

_____

_____

8. When was the last time you over-delivered on something…and did so joyfully? What was it, and why did you work so hard to make it happen?

_____

_____

_____

_____

9. When was the last time you were in a state of flow and in the zone, and you totally lost track of time? What were you doing?

_____

_____

_____

_____

10. Imagine you won a huge fortune in the lottery. How would you spend the rest of your life? Would it be different than how you currently see your future unfolding?

_____
_____
_____
_____
_____

11. What would you do if you knew you could not fail?

_____
_____
_____
_____
_____

12. What topics do you find yourself passionately arguing or defending with others on a regular basis?

_____
_____
_____
_____
_____

13. What are you most afraid of for the next generation (whether you have kids or not)?

_____

_____

_____

_____

_____

14. What do you love helping people do? How do you most commonly help others?

_____

_____

_____

_____

_____

15. What's your favorite section in the bookstore? What's the first magazine you pick up at the newsstand?

_____

_____

_____

_____

_____

16. When was the last time you couldn't fall asleep because you were so excited about a project or event? What was it?

17. If you trusted that your art, writing, singing (i.e., your creativity) would support your life financially, how would you live? Richly, sparsely, where?

18. If you didn't need to work for income, where would you put your time and energy into contributing to society?

19. Of all the work roles you've had in your life, which one would you gladly do for free?

_____

_____

_____

_____

_____

20. If you were able to attend your own funeral, what would you want to hear people saying? What would you like your epitaph to say?

_____

_____

_____

_____

_____

21. What do you want to be remembered for? What mark do you want to leave on the world?

_____

_____

_____

_____

_____

22. What do your friends tell you you'd be good at and that you should do for a living? (i.e. "You'd make a great...")? If you don't remember, ask them.

_____

_____

_____

_____

_____

23. What are you naturally curious about?

_____

_____

_____

_____

_____

24. When you have a free hour to surf the Internet, what do you explore?

_____

_____

_____

_____

_____

25. Think back to when you were five or ten years old. What did you want to be when you grew up? What skills and metaphors do these represent? (I.e., "becoming a pilot" might represent freedom and exploration.)

_____

_____

_____

_____

26. If you could write a book to help the world—a book guaranteed to become a bestseller—what would the topic be and what would you title it?

_____

_____

_____

_____

27. What careers do you dream about? What jobs do others have that you wish were yours?

_____

_____

_____

_____

28. If you were to begin volunteering your time tomorrow, what cause or group would you choose?

_____

_____

_____

_____

_____

_____

29. What change do you want to see in the world? What revolution would you be proud to lead?

_____

_____

_____

_____

_____

_____

As you answered the questions, did you notice any patterns, similar responses, or repeated words, themes, and directions? Jot down your favorite answer(s) for each of the areas below. Look back through your answers, specifically focusing on common threads and responses that jump out at you or perhaps even give you an Aha moment.

a. What recurring theme do you notice about your uppermost desires? (See questions numbered: 7, 15, 20, 21, 26.) Jot down your favorite(s) here:

_____

_____

_____

_____

_____

b. What is the one thing—or the top two to three things—that you've always wanted, but perhaps have not (fully) made happen? (See questions numbered: 2, 20, 21, 23, 24.) Jot down your favorite(s) here:

_____

_____

_____

_____

_____

c. What are you really good at? (See questions numbered: 4, 5, 6, 8, 14, 22.) Jot down your favorite(s) here:

_____

_____

_____

_____

_____

d. What makes your heart race? What drives you? What are the *top* one to three of these you'd *really love* to spend your time on in the future? (See questions numbered: 1, 3, 8, 9, 10, 11, 12, 13, 14, 15, 16, 17, 18, 19, 26, 27, 28, 29.) Jot down your favorite(s) here:

_____

_____

_____

_____

_____

e. What successes have you had in the past? (See questions numbered: 4, 6, 8, 9, 14, 16, 19, 22.) Jot down your top favorite(s) here:

_____

_____

_____

_____

PUTTING IT ALL TOGETHER

Let's start by creating a clear *vision*—a direction in which you'd like to see your life moving. Take your answers from above, and insert them here: The answers from questions (a) and (b) above should fairly clearly reveal your *vision*:

_____

_____

_____

_____

Next, let's pinpoint your *passion*: Take a look at your answers in the section (d) above. What is your top item that stands out? It may very well point to your *passion*:

_____

_____

_____

_____

Lastly, let's identify your *top skills*. Take a look at your answers in the sections (c) and (e)—what is your top item that stands out?

_____

_____

_____

_____

Once you have a clear *vision*, know your top *passions*, and have pinpointed your top *skills*, you now have the formula to create your encore—your chosen purpose for the next chapter in your life.

The Formula to Find Your Encore

V Your **VISION** what you *want*

\+

P Your **PASSION** what you *like*

\+

SKW Your **SKILLS, KNOWLEDGE, & WISDOM** what you *have*

= **Your ENCORE**

The Formula to find your *encore*, your next big step in life

Keep in mind a few notes about the formula. It's broad and general, the answers are subjective, and you will likely see the answer you want to see. So work through it a few times over plugging in different elements, and see how that changes the answer. And while it's not the end-all, it's a tool to help steer you in the right direction.

YOUR VISION STATEMENT

Now let's start working on your vision statement. For example, if your top *desire* (a) is to feel free—perhaps to travel a lot, and the stand-out of your top *wants, goals, and dreams* (b) is to write a book on a topic that's close to your heart and then speak regularly in front of large crowds, then your vision statement could be:

"I'll spend the next years of my life traveling, hiking, climbing as many mountains as I can. I'll write at least an hour a day in my book on my Passion Topic. I'll volunteer to speak at conferences and events, and I will contact organizations that want to hear my presentations & keynotes."

Note: This is *your* vision statement, so it does not have to be pretty—it simply has to state what you'd love your life to look like during the many years you still have to walk this earth. Write your vision statement here:

_____

_____

_____

_____

_____

If you are not clear about your passion, that's okay. Keep digging, take the Passion Quiz again, and look for those little pictures that pop into your head when you daydream. Do a lot of daydreaming. It will come to you, and when it does, come back and plug it into the formula and create your vision statement.

Chapter 1: Visioning Your Dream

If you are clear about your passion and have a clear vision on how you want to spend the next few decades of your life, my challenge for you is to:

- *Commit* to transforming your vision to reality.
- *Plan*—Use an electronic or paper planner, and jot down small implementable steps that'll take you toward your vision.
- *Decide* to take *Action* on that plan.
- *Join Like-Minded People*—It's easier to make it happen if you do it together with others who are walking the same exploratory path.
- *Ask For Help* whenever needed, and offer to support others with your strengths. For the most part, people want to help each other, so give others a chance to mentor and support you.
- *Get an Accountability Partner or Coach*—Share your ideas and plans with someone, and enlist them to hold you accountable for making progress. Find someone who will help you stay motivated and overcome real or perceived obstacles standing in your way.

Now that you've spent some time envisioning yourself taking your next step, have engaged in the introspective Passion Quiz, and have written your vision statement, keep it in mind as a compass for your future efforts in this book. As an example, I will share with you the vision statement I used to guide me while planning for my sailing journey.

1. *"I will sail around the world and honor my mother in a big way."* *In fact, my sailboat was named after my mother, Julia.*

After six years and completing my circumnavigation, I needed a new vision statement. I struggled to find my encore, so I threw myself into writing my award-winning memoir, *The Boy Behind the Gate*. While writing, it dawned on me that I knew how to let go and find a new identity, and I could perhaps help others in their same quest. So I created this next vision statement.

2. *"I will help others identify and use their passion combined with their skills, expertise, and dreams to take their next big step toward their encore in life beyond their careers."*

Another way of saying it could have been, *"I help others cut their dock lines and leave the harbor."* It doesn't matter how you say it, so don't worry about making it perfect since you can always revise and strengthen this statement as you go along.

Congratulations! You have gone deep in identifying your passions, desires, and skills. Have you identified and envisioned your dream? If not, go back and repeat this chapter, or come back to it later.

CHAPTER 2
TURNING YOUR DREAMS INTO GOALS

My goal is to inspire you to make your dreams come true. Whatever your vision is, whatever your dream is, I hope you'll take away from this book the understanding of how to make your dreams a reality. Dreams come in all sizes, from small to big, and if it's your dream, then it's important. I know that small or big, dreams can be overwhelming. It's difficult to go from doctor to artist in one fell swoop, and downshifting from CEO to tending your roses is not an easy transition either. Keep in mind you don't have to sail all the way around the world to:

- Have an Adventure
- Fulfill a Dream
- Pursue Your Passion

Your encore doesn't have to be sailing around the world, climbing Mt. Everest, or becoming CEO of the next great company. You can derive fulfillment and purpose from many different parts of your life, and it could be something related or unrelated to your career. I know:

- an architect who now runs a pizza parlor
- a CEO who runs fishing charters
- a cop who teaches ethics
- an attorney who mentors troubled kids

And you don't have to be an expert at something to begin. You can learn along the way. It's important to keep your focus not on what you can't do, but on what you can do. If you want to learn to play guitar, pick up a guitar and start playing. Want to write? Are you writing?

To reduce the amount of overwhelm in making your small or large dream come true, you'll need to break the dream down into smaller segments. It's important to turn your dreams into achievable goals. You can envision a dream, but there's nothing tangible to grab onto to begin making it happen. When you break down a big goal into smaller goals, then put them all back together, you can achieve anything.

I'm not a big fan of sports metaphors, but football surely fits here. When you get the ball to a first down, you get another chance to go again. You don't have to run the entire hundred yards at once. In baseball, you just need to reach one base at a time. You can sail around the world one island or country at a time, and you can write a book one chapter at a time.

In this chapter, you will break your vision down into reasonable and achievable goals using the Action Guide. Over many years, I've developed what I believe is one of the most effective goal-achievement systems. There's probably a little bit of each of the great motivators in here, and I tip my hat to them. I have put them all together into a system that works.

WRITE THEM DOWN

The first part of what works is writing your goals down. *You must write them down.* It was ten years after I wrote my goals down on a yellow piece of paper that I sailed out the Golden Gate. I still have that paper on which I wrote, "In ten years I want to do two things:"

1. *"Cruise the South Pacific in my own boat at least fifty feet long."*

2. *"Honor my mother Julia in a significant way."*

There were other goals for one and five years, but these were the only two in my ten-year category. Those were both big dreams seemingly so broad I didn't know what to do first to make them a reality. So I started making lists of things I thought needed doing in order to make them happen. I looked at each of these categories: *career*, *income*, *home/relationship*, *security*, and *identity*, and broke them down, outlining my goals and my feelings about each.

- Next to *career,* I wrote, "sell company." I needed to sell my company in order to sail around the world.

- Next to *income,* I knew I had to take my investments into account in order to sustain myself while journeying around the world.

- For *home,* I had to consider if it was that important for me to walk away from a great twenty-year relationship.

- With respect to my *security,* I had to think about the trip itself. Would I return? Would I be safe?

- How about my *identity?* I'd worked for twenty years to build my reputation as a successful executive. Was I willing to let go of that to become a cruising sailor?

I kept breaking each category down further and further to the point of actual action steps I needed to take for each category. And that's what you're going to do. Except I'm making it much easier for you. The goal setting section in the Action Guide shows five columns:

- *Goal*
- *Resources*
- *Action Steps*
- *Risk*
- *Priority*

We're just going to focus on goals, resources, and action steps for now, and we'll assess priority and risk later in the book. There are multiple lines to write because your dream, your next big step, is made up of more than just one goal. Your vision will take multiple goals to make happen.

What people, knowledge, and other resources will you need? Obviously, I needed a boat. I also needed to take a diesel mechanics course, and I needed crew—and the lists began to build. What are the action steps you need to take?

The fun part is these organizational methods are probably not new to you. The change for you is using them not for your professional life, but for *you*. And believe it or not, even though they're the same, almost all of us have a hard time applying these disciplines to our personal lives. But as you did in your work career, trust the systems experts have established. Follow this goal-achievement technique, and even though it's a long, methodical strategy, investing the effort upfront is the key to succeeding. Sound like something you may have said to some people or learned during your career?

In the Action Guide, write down action items needed to achieve your goals. Then, beside your action item, write down the resources you'll need to accomplish each. This may take a bit of time; some say it's a tedious process, but it's important to have something tangible you can do toward your goals. Otherwise, your dream will always remain a dream.

ACTION GUIDE 2: CREATING ACHIEVABLE GOALS

"Neither words nor worry affect outcome, only action does."
—Larry Jacobson

Let's take some action and identify your *goals*. The form below gives a bird's eye view of each of your goals, as well as your analysis of each. To give you more space to write, I have broken the form into separate sets of questions for up to four goals. You may in actuality have more or fewer goals. Remember, these are the goals you need to accomplish to make your big dream become reality.

Using the form as your visual guideline, after you have identified each goal, write down measurable and reasonable *action steps* you'll need in order to accomplish each goal. Some of your goals might require more action steps than others.

Lastly, you'll assess the *resources* you have, or still need, in order to help you accomplish each action step. Resources could include people, money, time, and knowledge. You will be assessing the risks and priorities associated with each action step later in the book so leave those blank for now.

GOAL #1	ACTION STEPS	RESOURCES	RISKS	PRIORITIES A-D
Goal #1 Sail around the world	Example: Find out how someone else did it?			
	Buy a boat. Find the money.			
	Find crew.			
	Learn to navigate.			
GOAL #1	**ACTION STEPS**	**RESOURCES**	**RISKS**	**PRIORITIES**
Goal #2 Mentor entreprenuers	Find local entreprenuer clubs or classses at schools			

1. Goal Number 1: Write down the first goal you will need to accomplish in order to pursue your passion-filled retirement.

___

___

___

___

___

___

___

Chapter 2: Turning Your Dreams into Goals

2. Write down any number of measurable and achievable action steps you'll need to complete in order to achieve that goal.

_____

_____

_____

_____

_____

_____

_____

_____

3. Lastly, write down the resources you'll need in order to achieve each action step. Start with the resources you already have and add the ones you need to acquire.

_____

_____

_____

_____

_____

_____

_____

_____

4. Goal Number 2: Write down the next goal you will need to accomplish in order to pursue your passion-filled retirement.

_____

_____

_____

_____

_____

_____

_____

5. Now, write down any number of measurable and achievable action steps you'll need to complete in order to achieve that goal.

_____

_____

_____

_____

_____

_____

_____

6. Write down the resources you'll need in order to achieve each action step. Start with the resources you already have and add the ones you need to acquire.

_____

_____

_____

_____

_____

_____

_____

_____

7. Goal Number 3: Write down the next goal you will need to accomplish in order to pursue your passion-filled retirement.

_____

_____

_____

_____

_____

_____

_____

8. Now, write down any number of measurable and achievable action steps you'll need to complete in order to achieve that goal.

___

___

___

___

___

___

___

9. Write down the resources you'll need in order to achieve each action step. Start with the resources you already have and add the ones you need to acquire.

___

___

___

___

___

___

___

10. Goal Number 4: Write down your next big goal you will need to accomplish in order to pursue your passion-filled retirement.

_____

_____

_____

_____

_____

_____

_____

_____

11. Now, write down any number of measurable and achievable action steps you'll need to complete in order to achieve that goal.

_____

_____

_____

_____

_____

_____

_____

12. Lastly, write down the resources you'll need in order to achieve each action step. Start with the resources you already have and add the ones you need to acquire.

_____

_____

_____

_____

_____

_____

_____

Well done on completing chapter two. I know it required a lot of introspection and soul-searching, but I'm confident you made it through unscathed. We have all been setting goals our entire lives, but this time was different for you. I simplified a complex process by asking you to break down each goal into smaller action steps required to achieve that goal. You then explored the resources available to you—or some you might still need—to help with each goal.

Later in the book, we'll return to examine the priority and risk of each of these goals. I ask that you trust the system. Because you're doing this work now, by the end of the book, you'll end up with a plan of action that is doubt-free. You'll know exactly what you want, as well as the steps necessary to get there, all due to the work you're doing now.

Did you establish achievable goals with action steps and identify the resources you'll need? If you haven't yet, please take the time to do this important step in the process, as it will be the foundation for much of what we'll do in the upcoming chapters.

CHAPTER 3

YOUR PERSONAL SWOT ANALYSIS

When I announced to my family and friends I was going to quit my career to sail around the world, the advice, opinions, and questions flooded in from all points of the compass. For example, "You can't go, you don't have any ocean sailing experience!" "You can't go, what about your job?" "How will you pay your taxes, what will you do with your car, will you close your cellular phone account? You don't have crew. Do you know how to navigate? Can I have your bicycle?" And they kept coming. I listened and realized the advice was coming in four categories. I was being handed a personal SWOT analysis by people who had no qualifications to analyze my situation, and they were giving knee-jerk reactions.

SWOT, as you may know, is a tool used to measure *strengths, weaknesses, opportunities* and *threats.* As I was gearing up for my sailing trip, this is what the SWOT analysis looked like through the voices of friends and family.

- *Strengths*: Some people said, "Good luck, we know you can do it, you have tenacity."

- *Weaknesses*: Many people said, "You don't have the experience, you'll get hurt, and you won't make it past New Zealand." (New Zealand is where most sailors from the West Coast of the US end their journey.)

- *Opportunities*: A few people said, "When opportunity knocks, you'd better be there to answer the door. If you can make this happen, go for it!"

- *Threats*: One of my brothers said, "You are going to die! Are you nuts?!"

So I made my own SWOT analysis, and in the end I decided I did have the perseverance I thought would be needed. I accepted I did not have the necessary experience.

I knew this was *the opportunity* I had dreamed of for so long. If I didn't go then, I probably would never do it. And I figured that if I died, it would be a heck of a way to go.

When I summarized, I ended up with tenacity, passion, and the fact that this was my one chance. I decided these strengths would carry me through the weaknesses and threats, and I was right.

As you may know from your professional life, a SWOT analysis can be very helpful in assessing your current position and identifying potential obstacles in order to set yourself up for success. It's often used to analyze a company's potential. By looking at your *strengths*, *weaknesses*, *opportunities*, and *threats* here, you can analyze the potential of bringing your vision to fruition. In this chapter, you will conduct your own personal SWOT analysis and learn how to both leverage your strengths and opportunities and overcome your weaknesses and threats.

Strengths: Do you feel you're good enough? Deserving of this? Do you have unique skills from your career or other professional skills? The same traits, skills, and characteristics you used to get where you are now, plus new skills you learn, are what you'll use to get where you want to go tomorrow. My guess is you already have the perseverance, or you wouldn't be where you are today. And you have the ability to learn new skills in case you don't have the knowledge you need to move forward.

One of my biggest strengths is perseverance. I learned it in sales when making cold calls. So when we were caught in a storm at sea, I knew we would make it through—I knew I could persevere. I have been a lifelong student, always pursuing new knowledge, and I calculated that as a strength. I knew I could eventually learn what knowledge was needed, and I figured there was no way I could know everything necessary before leaving. If I waited to know it all, I'd never leave. I discovered you don't have to be an expert to begin something, you can learn as you go. I also had good organizational skills learned from business, which came in handy when managing boat rebuilding projects.

Weaknesses: Do you have guilt about reaching for your dream? Do you need to forgive yourself for past actions in order to feel you deserve this? Do you feel selfish for doing this? Do you feel ill-prepared? Do you have the support of your family and friends? Do you have the knowledge? Are you okay with leaving your current identity behind? Even though I had been sailing since I was age thirteen, I only had one ocean crossing under my belt. And while my father had encouraged me to take auto mechanic shop in high school, I didn't listen to him, so I had a lot of learning about engines ahead of me. I calculated my lack of knowledge as a weakness, yet my quest for learning as a strength.

Opportunities and Connections: Yes, I added connections to this category. What resources can you leverage? Is there a particular opportunity because of the current market or trends in popular culture? Do you have a network to support you, perhaps one you have built through years of networking events? Is there a need in your community? Do you dream about flying across the country in your own private plane and happen to know an airline pilot who can advise you? I had a good enough credit rating to get a loan for my boat. I had a wonderful partner who handled all aspects of my personal life while I was gone. And I was in good physical condition. Along with good timing, these were my opportunities. I felt if I didn't go then, I couldn't see it happening in the distant future.

Threats: Are there reasons you haven't started or aren't making progress? Do you foresee particular obstacles in your future? In my case, there were many threats or reasons not to go. Fear was in the air since 9/11 had just occurred and the world was a scary place. I had never navigated or captained a boat across a three-thousand-mile-wide ocean before, I was going to be spending all of my money, I was committing career suicide and cutting off my income. I was going into the unknown, leaving security behind in my wake. I was leaving my home, my friends, and my family, and I didn't know if or when I would ever see them again. But for me the hardest thing of all to face was leaving my identity behind. I was a fast-paced executive running around the Silicon Valley and had built an excellent reputation for the company and myself. Now I was going to be a sailor, which to most people is equal to a hitchhiking hobo. I truly had to weigh my SWOT analysis and cast aside the longest lists, which were the threats and weaknesses.

> There was no logic in what I was doing. The left side of my brain was screaming, "Are you nuts? This makes no sense!" But the right side of my brain, the side that is filled with passion, desire, quest, and images of grandeur, won out. Because it turns out that passion wins over all, if you let it.

There are some items you'll want to keep in mind:

- Where do your finances fit into your SWOT analysis? Can you afford to do what you want? Talk to your financial advisor.

- What about your social life? Do you have enough friends and hobbies? Do you want more? Does that play into what you want to do or where you want to go?

- How is your health? Are you in healthy enough condition to do what you want to do?

Now it's your turn. Conduct your own SWOT analysis, category by category, by recording your thoughts in the Action Guide.

ACTION GUIDE 3A: BRING IN THE SWOT TEAM

You have now learned how you can adapt a SWOT analysis to help you achieve your goals. While the chart gives you an overall picture of the analysis, you may find it easier to write your answers below the actual questions.

STRENGTHS	WEAKNESSES

OPPORTUNITIES	THREATS

1. Brainstorm your strengths and list them below:

_____

_____

_____

_____

_____

_____

_____

_____

_____

2. Brainstorm your weaknesses and list them below:

_____

_____

_____

_____

_____

_____

_____

_____

_____

3. Brainstorm your opportunities and connections and list them below:

_____

_____

_____

_____

_____

_____

_____

_____

_____

4. Brainstorm your threats on the way to achieving your plan and list them below:

_____

_____

_____

_____

_____

_____

_____

_____

Now that you've assessed your own SWOT, come up with three things in each category you can do to either overcome your weaknesses and threats or leverage your strengths and opportunities. For example, before departing, my knowledge of diesel engines consisted of knowing that a mouse ran around in circles chasing cheese and that turned the propeller. So I took a diesel mechanics class. It gave me the basics but didn't even come close to the knowledge I ended up needing while at sea. It was, however, a start.

I had owned but had never been an official captain of a boat and didn't then hold a USCG captains license as I now do. I didn't know how to read weather maps or navigate, and these were definite weaknesses. But I learned as we went because I was used to continually learning.

> Remember, you don't have to be an expert to try something. You can become the expert as you go.

Would additional education serve your goals? If you'd like to be a painter, but you've never had a formal painting lesson, might you consider enrolling in a class? Or do you think devoting time to practice and self-study is better suited to your lifestyle? Either way, it's good to identify educational weaknesses and commit to devoting time to bridge any gaps.

You may also be able to repurpose your career skills. From my business experience, I had good leadership skills for managing people, and that turned out to be very important on a boat with anywhere from one to five crew on board.

Take a look at the weaknesses and threats you've identified. Have you learned any skills in your career that can be repurposed to overcome these potential obstacles?

ACTION GUIDE 3B: MANAGE YOUR WEAKNESSES AND CAPITALIZE ON YOUR STRENGTHS

In your SWOT analysis, go back and add the "buts." In other words, if a weakness is lack of knowledge, add "but I can learn as I go." If a weakness is your income slowing or stopping, add "but I can sell some assets," or "I can work along the way." If a weakness is a fear of no longer being the one in charge, add "but now I'll be the one in charge of me." You get the idea. Add the "buts."

Add your "buts" here:

_____

_____

_____

_____

_____

_____

_____

Let's now look at the other side and identify actions you can take to capitalize on your strengths and opportunities. For example, maybe your large network of career colleagues is one of your strengths, and you know someone who can help propel you toward your big dream.

Add how you will leverage your strengths and opportunities here:

_____

_____

_____

_____

_____

_____

_____

_____

_____

_____

_____

_____

Congratulations! You've successfully conducted a SWOT analysis, and you're setting yourself up for success by identifying your strengths and exploiting them. You also know your weaknesses and how to overcome them.

There'll be no stopping you now.

CHAPTER 4
ELEMENTS OF A BALANCED LIFESTYLE

We have been working to find your one great passion, and hopefully more than just that one. The scale of your dreams and the challenges inherent in realizing them will affect how many other interests you can maintain in your life. My sailing journey around the world is a good example of what I mean.

I had a one-track mind for three years before my sailing journey, and then for six more years abroad during the circumnavigation. I was solely focused on sailing and achieving my lifelong dream of sailing all the way around the world. Every action I took, every thought I had, every conversation I engaged in was about sailing. I was either telling a sailing adventure story myself or asking about fixing equipment, the weather, finding out more information about our next destination, or listening to another sailor's story.

At the time, it seemed so interesting to me, and for the most part, it was all I cared about in thought and action. I was eager to absorb the wealth of information available in order to achieve my goal, and I was completely immersed. Looking back now, I must have been a pretty boring person to engage with unless you wanted to talk sailing, anchorages, weather, and visa requirements in foreign countries. I recognize that for me, it was the only way I could stay focused on such a huge project—to throw myself into it 100 percent because I felt I didn't want to be distracted by anything else. *Julia* was my home, and I needed to do all I could to keep her afloat and in good working order at all times. Therefore, I focused on things like learning how to forecast the weather as well as how to install an engine alternator, experimenting with various ways of setting the sails, maintaining contact with other boats going our direction via ham radio, and keeping up with the latest entry requirements to other countries as the world. I was also experiencing a fear newly introduced into everyone after 9/11, all while trying to stretch my budget to ensure I could make it all the way around the world.

While I still believe in having a primary passion and following it, I now advocate living a more balanced life. From my work with coaching clients, I have found the happiest ones are those living a well-balanced life with multiple interests and activities. Thus, I created *Your Retirement Wheel*, and I invite you to evaluate your areas of interest to see how well-balanced a life you are leading.

Creating and living a fulfilling retirement depends on balancing multiple areas of your life. One of the main "secrets" to creating that "perfect" retirement is to identify which areas of your life are at the level you desire, and which still need some improvement. I have selected eight areas of life I feel are key to well-balanced living. You may want to add areas to the wheel which are of high importance to you. For now, let's jump right in and begin the balancing act.

ACTION GUIDE 4A: YOUR RETIREMENT WHEEL

In this exercise, we'll identify those areas of your life with which you are satisfied, and those which can be improved. Remember that change requires action, from small steps to giant leaps, to bring about the modification you seek. Below is a powerful tool that will help you identify your level of satisfaction in eight very important areas of your life.

Your ultimate goal is to achieve balance in the eight areas listed on the wheel. Rate each of the eight areas on the spokes of the wheel, with "1" being the lowest level of satisfaction and "5" meaning you are very satisfied in that area.

Once you have rated each area, draw a line connecting your ratings on the eight spokes of the wheel. This will give you a great visual of what is working well in your life, and what needs new effort in order to achieve your vision of a balanced retirement.

YOUR RETIREMENT WHEEL™

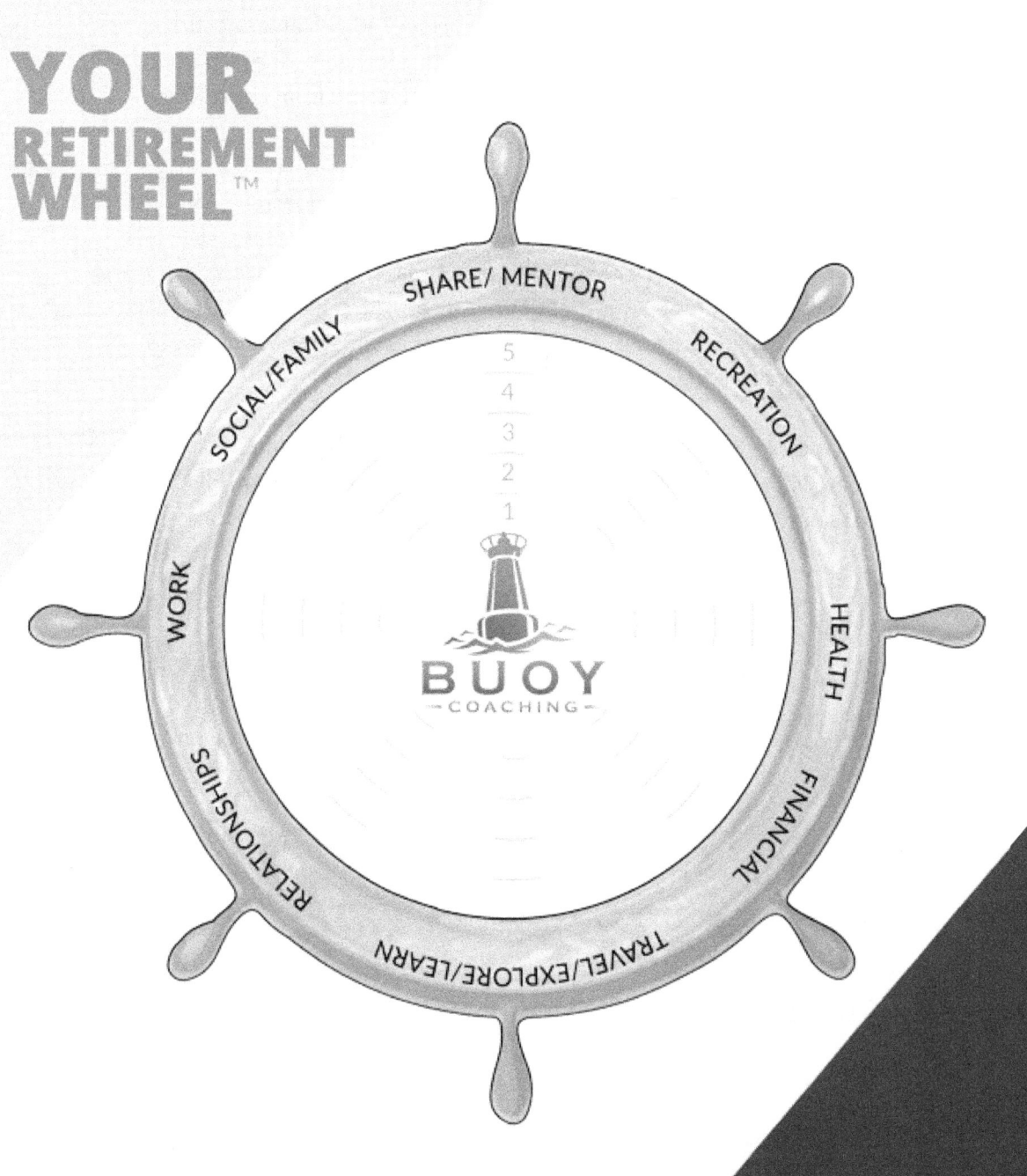

How does your wheel look? Is it balanced? Does your wheel look like it would roll smoothly down the road or is it lopsided? Which areas need work? Are any of the spokes that you rated with a low number really important to you? Can you identify what is stopping you from improving those areas?

I understand just your knowing what you need to change doesn't mean you'll do it. Being aware of areas you'd like to improve is the *first* step in making any changes you need or want in your life. It's the old "Easier said than done" syndrome. But that doesn't mean you can't begin to take action and actually work on it. Small steps are fine, and if it's important to you, then there's no reason to put it off any longer.

The good news is, that's exactly what we are working on—helping you create your actionable steps. Then it'll be up to you to implement those steps.

ACTION GUIDE 4B: FINDING YOUR BALANCE

SOLO OR TOGETHER?

This is not relationship counseling, but if you live with a spouse, partner, friend, or long-term roommate, you may wish to consider if he or she shares your vision of retirement. If so, that's a strength, and you can work together toward your goals. But there's a chance he or she may not share your exact same passion.

If you are living together, it doesn't mean you must share all of the same interests or spend all of your time together. A good sign of a great relationship is encouraging each other in your individual pursuits, even if they're completely different from your own interests. You might want to consider how to bring your spouse or partner on board with your vision. Perhaps the two of you can merge your visions, possibly modifying yours if needed.

For example, while you may wish to take a world cruise for a year, your spouse or partner might be uncomfortable at sea and would be pushing their limits just to go to sea for a week. Perhaps you could come to a compromise on taking a calm river cruise in Europe.

Hopefully your visions intersect at least in some areas and you can spend time pursuing some areas of your passion together. Beyond that, you can express your love and respect by supporting each other's areas of interest with curiosity and active listening—a skill that for many of us takes some serious practice. It's important to understand where the other person comes from and how they see your interests. When discussing your hopeful plans, take the time to listen to what they say about how this will affect them and your relationship.

You may find your relationship falls under both strength and weakness in your SWOT analysis. The key is to communicate with each other—ideally taking turns expressing yourselves, and truly listening with an open mind to the other's ideas, goals, and vision.

FLYING SOLO

For those not currently in a relationship, you even get your own category known as Solo Agers. Up to this point, everything applies to you as well as those partnered. The difference now is you don't have to explain yourself to anyone. That can be a plus, although it can also be a minus as it leaves you without someone who knows you well to discuss your ideas and plans. Many of my coaching clients are Solo Agers, and I am there for them as an active listener sounding board. I suggest everyone needs somebody to run things by and to hold them accountable.

We're about to dig into the categories on the Retirement Wheel, and some that aren't on the wheel. But first, more questions for you.

YOUR LIVING SITUATION

Ask yourself the following questions. Be honest with yourself as the purpose is self-discovery.

Do you like your current living situation? Do you like the location, living space, and neighbors? Is it convenient for shopping, dining, and the activities in which you participate? Is it close enough (or far enough) from your family? Is it too densely populated or not urban enough? Is it affordable on your retirement budget? Write a few notes here:

_____

_____

_____

If all is good, then your living situation is a strength. If not, it may be a weakness upon which you need to improve. In general, are you pleased with your current living situation or are you feeling the need to change things up a bit?

On a scale of 1 to 5, rate your satisfaction with your living situation: 1 meaning you are completely dissatisfied; 5 signifying you are completely satisfied. Circle one.

1   2   3   4   5

YOUR FINANCES

This is not a book about the financial aspects of your retirement. However, I do suggest you keep the following in mind as you vision your future.

Are your finances a strength or weakness, an opportunity or a threat? Are you able to live the lifestyle you want with your current and projected finances? If so, consider that a strength. If not, then it's a weakness or threat, and part of your plan may include earning money part or full time. If you want to retire on a cruise ship, can you afford it? That goes for any big change in lifestyle such as moving, travel, education, or starting a business. If you can't afford what you want, you have three choices. You can either:

1. Modify your desired lifestyle.

or

2. Continue making money by working part or full time.

or

3. Win the lottery (Don't count on this).

On a scale of 1 to 5, rate your satisfaction with your finances: 1 meaning you are completely dissatisfied; 5 signifying you are completely satisfied. Circle one.

1   2   3   4   5

SHARING YOUR KNOWLEDGE AND WISDOM

Throughout your life you have been accumulating knowledge, skills, experience, and tricks of the trade from your profession. You may also have this same information relating to your hobby, recreational, or other activities. What will happen to all of this wisdom when you retire and are no longer involved in a daily exchange of information? Will yours be lost forever…or will you somehow pass it on to others? Without experiences and knowledge being passed on to others, yours will not be recorded and will disappear when you do. I know it's sad to think about letting your precious experience go to waste, so let's make sure that doesn't happen.

How will you share your knowledge and wisdom with the world?

HOW TO SHARE YOUR WISDOM

- You can teach at your local college continuing education program, at night school; substitute at day schools; assist at private schools; offer workshops through meet-up groups; create a course and put it up on sites like Udemy.com; or give a talk at your local Rotary, Lions Club, or other clubs and organizations to which you belong. You might even take this opportunity to work on becoming a professional speaker. The sky is the limit.

- Mentor kids, entrepreneurs, and students in your field. Be a golf mentor at the public course or at your private club. Be a big brother or sister. Opportunities abound to be a mentor or even a consultant, either for pay or just because you want to help people.

- Coach kids or adult sports teams or other leagues, from card playing to pickleball, from chess playing to fashion design.

- A great way to share your knowledge is through writing. You can publish your own book or report on Kindle, and you can find all the information you need about the simple process at KDP or IngramSpark.

- You can write about any subject and as often as you like by publishing online with a blog. There's lots of information available online about how to get started with blogging. It's the modern-day version of "shouting from the rooftops."

See the Resources Page on the www.BuoyCoaching.com website for more ideas, including many volunteer options.

SHARING/MENTORING

On a scale of 1 to 5, rate your satisfaction with "sharing your knowledge as an aspect of your life: 1 meaning you are completely dissatisfied; 5 signifying you are completely satisfied.

        1   2   3   4   5

WORK

Are you considering staying active in your field and earning a living? You can do so by leveraging your knowledge, skills, and experience. What do you know how to do best? What have you learned in your professional experience that you would like to continue with further work?

_____

_____

_____

_____

_____

_____

How much of a supplemental paycheck do you need? Can you earn this without having to work the long hours of your professional career?

_____

_____

_____

_____

_____

_____

Keep in mind one of your primary goals is to create balance in your retirement. During our professional careers, we tend to be out of balance by giving a disproportionate amount of time to work. Make it a priority to create balance in your life.

However, work can be for purposes beyond just earning money. Chances are your professional life also provided you with fulfillment and purpose. You were *needed*, *valued*, *respected*, and *you were a contributor.* You were given feedback and advice, scolded, and thanked—and you gave all of that back to others. You were socially interactive at work.

This fulfillment—this feeling of belonging to something larger than yourself and being valued for your experience—is what you want to look for in a job search, whether it is for full or part time employment.

Maybe financial gain is not a priority, in which case you can spend your time serving others and sharing your knowledge and experience while feeling valued and needed. Volunteering for your favorite organization will give you great satisfaction. Experiment with a few different positions and see what sits well with you.

If you were to do some sort of work in your retirement—either full or part time—what would be the perfect job, business, or volunteer opportunity?

_____

_____

_____

_____

_____

_____

_____

_____

_____

_____

See the Resources Page on the Buoy Coaching website for suggestions of where to look for opportunities.

What is your current satisfaction with your work and/or volunteering? On a scale of 1 to 5, rate your satisfaction with work as an aspect of your life: 1 meaning you are completely dissatisfied; 5 signifying you are completely satisfied.

1   2   3   4   5

RECREATION

Who says retirement can't be fun? This is your chance to spend plenty of time perfecting your golf swing, rekindle your tennis game, take up pickleball, become a champion card player, participate in a road rally, get back in the pool, take up yoga, and do those day hikes you've been talking about for so long.

Participation in and viewing of sports—from joining a softball league to following your local team around the country—can provide satisfaction, laughter, and smiles. I can't emphasize enough how important laughter is to your well-being. And staying active both mentally and physically is important to your long-term health and happiness.

While some people may think of watching television as recreational and fun, the fact is that sitting in front of it for an average of four and a half hours per day, as most retirees do, will not only steal those precious hours from your life, it will rob you of time you could use for physical and social activities. If you get in the habit of plunking yourself down in front of the TV midday and calling it 'resting,' there's a good chance that's where you'll stay.

> We are all subject to Newton's Law: A body in motion stays in motion, and a body at rest stays at rest. Commit to keeping yourself in motion.

On a scale of 1 to 5, rate your satisfaction with your recreation activities: 1 meaning you are completely dissatisfied; 5 signifying you are completely satisfied. Circle one.

1   2   3   4   5

If your number was 3 or below, consider the following six questions:

1. What new recreational activity have you longed to do, but have not yet acted on?

   _____

   _____

   _____

   _____

   _____

2. What activity have you stopped because of your professional life and would like to reactivate?

   _____

   _____

   _____

   _____

   _____

3. Which of these activities—from either number 1 or number 2 above—do you commit to starting today? Okay, or perhaps starting tomorrow. List it—or them—below.

   _____

   _____

   _____

4. What type of accessories or gear do you need to get started? When can you get them? Can it be sooner rather than later?

___

5. Do you want someone to join you? Who?

___

6. When will you get started?

___

HEALTH

We hear it from all directions. Our doctors, friends, family members, and the publications we read all tell us to "stay healthy." Yes, thank you, we know to keep our blood pressure down, to exercise, and to eat well, so I don't need to repeat it here. I can however offer ideas that are easy to implement with your newfound time in retirement.

We all know eating well is crucial to staying healthy. During our professional careers, we sometimes sacrificed quality for how quickly we could gobble down a meal and then get back to work. Now that those rushed days are behind you, this is your opportunity to focus on eating healthy, less processed foods and taking good care of your body. You can take the time to shop for healthier foods and spend more time cooking with those nutritious ingredients. You can also follow up on those missed doctors' appointments for the checkups he or she has recommended.

On a scale of 1 to 5, rate your satisfaction with your health: 1 meaning you are completely dissatisfied; 5 signifying you are completely satisfied. Circle one.

1   2   3   4   5

How will you take advantage of your abundance of time to improve your health? What will you do more of? What will you do less of?

_____

_____

_____

_____

_____

TRAVEL

Nearly everyone wants to travel, and retirement gives you the time to explore those places you've always wanted to visit. From cruising on a sailboat or cruise ship to traveling in a motor home or hotel hopping, and from adventure travel in a foreign land to being a tourist in your own city, the possibilities are endless.

Keep in mind that travel can be tiring and that it's not uncommon to bite off more than you can chew. More time in fewer destinations lets you absorb more of your surroundings. A series of small trips to explore places closer to home can also be rewarding, and not as exhausting as touring the world.

Plan ahead, work out your budget, and go!

On a scale of 1 to 5, rate your satisfaction with traveling as an aspect of your life: 1 meaning you are completely dissatisfied; 5 signifying you are completely satisfied. Circle one.

1   2   3   4   5

Whatever your number is, consider these six questions:

1. Where would you like to travel?

_____

_____

_____

_____

_____

2. How would you like to travel to that destination (cruise, fly, drive, RV, etc.)?

   _____

   _____

   _____

   _____

   _____

3. Does your spouse or partner have the same desires?

   _____

   _____

   _____

   _____

   _____

4. When would you be able to travel to that destination?

   _____

   _____

   _____

   _____

   _____

5. Is it within your budget?

___

6. What steps can you take right now to start planning this trip? For example, research, start a travel fund, put it on your calendar, talk to your travel agent, and so on.

LEARN—AND EXERCISE YOUR BRAIN

Our brains are muscles that need exercise just like our bodies. Learning is a great way to keep your mind active, alert, and sharp. Since you are reading this, we already know you are a person who understands the benefits of learning. What would you like to learn?

How about learning pottery or how to paint, going back to school to get a degree or just to study philosophy, or joining an astronomy club? Look up the courses offered by your local college and you'll see subjects that will surely spark your interest. There are also many options for online learning. Going back to school, either in person or virtually, is fun: You study the subjects you want, you meet new people, and it gives you purpose.

What is the next book and subject you want to study after this one?

_____

_____

_____

_____

_____

On a scale of 1 to 5, how would you rate your satisfaction with learning in your life: 1 meaning you are completely dissatisfied; 5 signifying you are completely satisfied. Circle one.

1   2   3   4   5

STAYING SOCIAL

During your professional career, most likely you socialized with others at work. Without the socializing that comes from your professional life, it falls on you to make the extra effort to remain connected to others.

Staying social is important because it keeps up our human interaction skills, such as getting along with others and maintaining a sense of ease with meeting new friends, and it makes us keep our hair and clothes looking sharp. It keeps us from lying around on the sofa in a purple velvet track suit in front of the TV nibbling chips.

You may also wish to spend more time with family such as your spouse or partner, siblings, children, and grandchildren. But while some people would love to become a permanent babysitter of the grandkids, to others that sounds a bit too much. Either answer is correct, and it's your choice.

Consider these questions:

How will you replace the social network you had in your professional life?

_____

_____

_____

_____

_____

What groups will you join?

_____

_____

_____

_____

_____

Where will you meet and stay connected with other people? If you're not sure, just list some options for now.

_____

_____

_____

_____

_____

Do you want more time (or less) with family? What specific effort can you make to reach out for more (or less) interaction?

_____

_____

_____

_____

_____

On a scale of 1 to 5, rate your satisfaction with staying social as an aspect of your life: 1 meaning you are completely dissatisfied; 5 signifying you are completely satisfied. Circle one.

1   2   3   4   5

RELATIONSHIPS

This book is by no means meant to be relationship counseling. However, I cannot emphasize enough the importance of relationships in our overall happiness in life. Studies (including the big Harvard study) show that having good relations with your spouse or partner, your friends, and your family is key to continual happiness. The Harvard study emphasized it is not necessarily your spouse or partner who matters—your friends are equally important. See the TED talk on this by Robert Waldinger on YouTube.

Being partnered or married takes effort from both parties, and good solid friendships also take work to keep them alive. I suggest you do the work, as nothing else will make you happier. That being said, answer these questions honestly. Yes, there is some overlap between this category and the previous one of staying social, but relationships are perhaps more personal.

Are you partnered or married? If so, how is your relationship going? Is it wonderful every day, or is it getting stale? What do you need to spice it up?

_____

_____

_____

_____

_____

_____

_____

If you're not in a relationship, do you want to be? Are you lonely often? Where can you put yourself out there to meet someone?

_____

_____

_____

_____

_____

What do you need to do to improve your relationships with your partner, friends, and family? Do you need to reach out more? Schedule regular calls? More visits?

_____

_____

_____

_____

_____

On a scale of 1 to 5, rate your satisfaction with relationships as an aspect of your life: 1 meaning you are completely dissatisfied; 5 signifying you are completely satisfied. Circle one.

1   2   3   4   5

AND NOW, A WORD FROM YOUR COACH

There are three things you need to retire:

1. *Something from which to retire.*

2. *Something to which you retire.*

3. *Someone to nag you to get off your duff and do it. Who will that be in your life?*

If you'd like to have a personal coach hold you accountable for taking action and balancing Your Retirement Wheel, contact me and we'll explore how I can help you. Many find that going it alone is not easy and that having an accountability partner is the quickest and most effective way to achieve all your personal or professional goals.

As you search for a balanced lifestyle, do you see in what areas you need to focus on in order to improve your life balance? Jot down what you need to work on.

_____

_____

_____

_____

_____

_____

_____

How balanced is your life? How balanced will it be with some changes you'd like to make? Try to keep a balanced life, and you'll find your day-to-day living more fulfilling.

CHAPTER 5

RISK ANALYSIS

"No risk, no reward." Surely you have heard that before. When faced with a risk, do you take the risk and seek the reward? Or does the risk scare you away? All great achievements require some sort of uncertainty, and therefore risk. More than likely, you'll have to let go of something in order to achieve your biggest goals. You dipped your toe into this in your goal setting, but this is a crucial part of taking your next step.

> Once you have truly analyzed the risks associated with your goals, your comfort level and confidence will skyrocket.

You didn't make it through your career without taking risks. Risks are trade-offs. How many evenings at home did you give up in favor of the office? You risked missing that time at home with your family, partner, or friends. You may have attended off-site company meetings held on weekends, causing you to miss your child's Saturday soccer games. You took the risk of missing the game because your passion drove you and you recognized you had to make sacrifices.

The world of risk hasn't changed much, though some consider the possibility of working from home in today's high-tech environment to be less risky. But there will always be some risk in whatever you do, including your encore beyond your work career. The project you have in mind might not work. Your art might not sell. Your book might not be interesting to a publisher. You might not be noticed in the way you may have been before.

Being a player in the corporate incentive travel industry, I was important enough to major hotels and airlines to merit free rooms and travel. Now I joke when I go into those same hotels and say, "Do you know who I used to be?" The recognition is long gone, along with my identity. I knew I was risking losing both when I left to go sailing, and I was right…I lost them.

However, the trade-off to become someone else and explore a whole new life was worth it a hundred times over. I've never looked back and always considered myself fortunate to get a "do-over." Remember playing baseball or another game as a kid and the ball would go out of bounds, or someone would *claim* it had gone out of bounds, and you couldn't agree? So someone would shout "Do-over!" And you got to make the play over again. How cool is that? That you get a "do-over" is an amazing *opportunity*. Don't pass it up by defaulting to just doing what you know because it's what you've been doing for so long. Don't confuse what your left brain knows with what your right brain wants.

I love this quote and have lived by it for years:

> "Man cannot discover new oceans unless he has the courage to lose sight of the shore."
> —Andre Gide

Another way to put it is,

> "You can't steal second base unless you take your foot off of first."
> —Multiple

Are you ready to steal second base? Are you ready to discover new oceans? You are the one who gets to decide what you're willing to risk for your goals. In this chapter, you will identify the risks associated with each step of your goals. You'll also weigh the risks according to *benefits, drawbacks, effects,* and *results*.

Do you know what the number one obstacle is to achieving your greatest dreams? It's not money, it's not time, and it's not anything you don't have. It's what you *do have*.

The good things in our lives are what get in the way of great things.

The trappings of success often tempt us to set aside our dreams in favor of the security we already enjoy. Perhaps you would like to move abroad for a year to write, but your life here is good, comfortable, and secure, and you can't see leaving it all behind. You have children or grandchildren, cars, a house, a job, club memberships, and responsibilities that keep you evenly happy. There's golf on Saturdays, yoga on Thursday evenings, and the grandkids' soccer tournaments. Are these good aspects of your life bursting the bubble of your biggest dreams?

If you can't see giving up some of those things, you might not experience living high on top of a hill in an Italian villa writing your great novel. Or if you're too concerned about who will watch the dog, that might hamper an around the world photography trip. You get to set the rules though. Maybe you compromise and take photographs from your Italian villa and bring the dog with you. You get to decide.

Some people are more used to taking risks than others. I took a big risk to start our company. I had been working for another company, and when that situation became intolerable, I had no choice but to leave. I took a huge risk going out on my own. But there's something to taking a risk and putting everything on the line. I was forced to succeed. Certainly, there's more pressure to succeed. I had a mortgage to pay, so I got up and went to work and focused. I made success happen.

You know what this is like. Chances are good you are already a risk-taker of some degree in your professional life. You didn't get to where you are without taking risks, but most of those risks were for the good of the company or your career. It's a completely different story when you consider taking those same types of risks for yourself. Can you do it? The best way to find out is by identifying and then weighing each of the risks in your Action Guide. Then stare at them for a while and picture what it would be like taking each risk.

I thought long and hard about taking the risks involved in sailing around the world. I didn't know anybody else who had just walked away—or sailed away—from his or her life as I was about to do. Therefore, I had no role model to follow and no inspirational story to motivate me. All I had was my passion, tenacity, and the good organizational skills I'd learned in business.

After twenty years in the corporate world, I decided to go for it. And this time, it would be for my personal passion. I had been dreaming of sailing around the world my entire life (well, at least since I was age thirteen when I first learned to sail). I simply had to try. I felt if I didn't try to make this happen, I would be letting myself down. I didn't know how I could face myself in the mirror if I didn't at least make the effort.

The odds were certainly against succeeding. Only about sixty people a year worldwide succeed in completing a circumnavigation because it's that difficult. However, once I decided, the experience of preparing for the journey was like being on a runaway freight train careening down the tracks at high speed. I became so immersed and dedicated, I couldn't stop my momentum toward the first goal of actually departing. There are lots of sailors who say they're going to go cruising but never do. I was determined not to be one of them. The total immersion was a wonderful experience. I had been that dedicated before for business, but doing it for me was a whole new ball of wax. I was blinded by it. And as someone who has previously achieved success in life, you too will be blinded by your desire to succeed again—this time for you.

Because I didn't have an inspirational story or role model to follow, I am determined to be that for you. My story is proof that anyone can make his or her grandest dreams come true. Part of that story is that I took huge risks. For a moment, think about what I left behind and what I risked to make my dream come true.

I left my twenty-year *career* behind: The day I sailed out the Golden Gate, I committed career suicide. I was gone for six years—so long that my clients had moved on, become consultants on their own, or were no longer in a buyer's position. To go back into the events and incentive travel industry would have meant starting all over again.

I left my *income*. I had a pretty good middle class income, and suddenly, it went to zero. I had just enough money to tease me into thinking I could afford the journey because I was able to get a boat loan. Even though I had sold my company, it was a service company and the value to the buyer was our clients, so we're not talking about selling a high-value tech company here. I figured I had enough money to last a couple of years, and then I didn't know what I would do. Want to talk about scary?

I left my *security*. By security, I mean everything from having a car in your driveway to the local grocer knowing your name. It's those familiar things, people, and events we surround ourselves with that make up our sense of security. I left it all behind for adventure. It would have been easy to stay home and continue with my good and secure life, but security wasn't what I was seeking. I was seeking adventure.

I left my *home*: not only my physical home, but also my friends and family. I didn't know when or if I would ever see any of them again. I was so focused on going that I never even considered the plan for return. Now I'm not suggesting you do that, as it was a very big risk and very scary. I tell you this to demonstrate I was aware of the risk and was willing to take it. I allowed the right side of my brain and the passion that lives there drive my decisions. And I'm glad I did.

Probably the most difficult of all was leaving my *identity*, letting go of who I was, who I had become, who I had built myself up to be as an executive in the fast-paced world, providing services to Silicon Valley and other high-profile companies in a wide variety of industries. I had built our company's reputation of being the best in the business, and I let go of it all. But I had a choice: Leave it all behind, or don't go. These were the things I had to leave behind to fulfill my dream.

Consider what you have to risk for your dream. Is it your identity? Your career? Home? Security? Income? There comes a time to move on, and perhaps, like me, you are ready to risk or let go of some elements of your life. I'm not suggesting you leave everything behind like I did, but you might have to let go of some things.

I have developed a system to assess any risks you are considering. Here, you'll write down the risk, and then consider the Benefits, Drawbacks, Effects, and Results if you do or don't take each risk. In this process, you bring your focus down to the reality of what it would be like moving forward with a particular risk, and it's very revealing.

For example, I left everything behind to sail around the world for six years.

Benefits: Among others, I achieved my lifelong dream and ended up feeling empowered, raised my self-esteem, gained a new perspective of the world, met new friends, became a better leader, and have a really cool story to tell, which I wrote about in the bestselling memoir, *The Boy Behind the Gate*.

I gained an enormous amount of knowledge about everything in *this* book. If I hadn't done it, I couldn't teach it, because I believe in teaching only from experience. And there are many more benefits too numerous to list.

Drawbacks: I spent nearly all of my savings and sold my house to fund the journey. That leaves me still more in need of earning a living than I had expected.

Effects: I am a changed person—for the better. I saw that the happiest people on earth are the ones who have the least. I discovered in myself how much I truly care about others and learned to be more interested in their well-being, which in turn makes me feel better about who I am. I gained the desire to give back to a society that has given so much to me. I gained a strong desire to coach others on how to do what I did.

Results: The results are that I finally know what it means to feel self-actualization because through my speaking, writing, and coaching, I am truly helping others realize their dreams.

In the spaces below, you'll find the place to put each risk, and alongside the risks, assess the potential benefits, drawbacks, effects, and results of each risk. To do this, you will most likely need to go back to your vision. Take a few minutes to revisit that vision and see the potential. This takes some thought, and quite frankly, most of what I discovered didn't occur to me before I went sailing out the Golden Gate. I discovered these things during the journey and after returning. So don't worry, you're not failing if you can't picture all of the potential from taking your next big step beyond your career.

The ultimate goal of this chapter is for you to understand that whatever you choose to do is associated with some sort of risk. Only you can evaluate if you're willing to take that risk. You could possibly minimize some of the risks. For example, I could have bought a smaller boat, which would have left me with a bit more money. I did consider that and made the choice not to buy a smaller boat. That wasn't part of my vision, and I wasn't willing to compromise. So I took the risk of spending more money.

Compare your risks with your vision. If you want to move to the Italian countryside to be a writer but aren't willing to give up your current home life, can you come up with other options? For example, can you rent a cottage in the California wine country? If you squint your eyes, it looks very much like rural Tuscany. Okay, you may have to squint hard, but I think you get the idea.

Compare the risks with your vision and determine which risks you're willing to take to make that vision a reality. Once you've decided which risks you're comfortable with, lock them in. Don't doubt your decision. Don't let others put doubts in your head. You've decided to take the risks—now become comfortable with them and the knowledge they will be part of your life. *Recognizing and understanding the risks you will take is key to having confidence in your venture.* This is an incredibly empowering gift you are giving yourself, one that can make or break your success in pursuing your vision.

Now that you've identified the risks associated with your goals and have decided on those with which you are comfortable, you can move forward.

Are you willing to take the risks you have identified—let go of some of the comfortable things in your life—and move toward your goals?

_____

_____

_____

_____

Are some of the positive aspects of your life keeping you from achieving great possibilities?

_____

_____

_____

Are you willing to break out of your comfort zone?

_____

_____

_____

Now that you've heard my story, you know somebody who has started his life over. We have all entertained ideas of reinventing ourselves, of having a chance to do it differently and by our own rules. There will be some risks involved, but if a regular guy named Larry did it, you can too.

ACTION GUIDE 5: RISK ANALYSIS

Now it's your turn. Refer back to the goals section in the Action Guide. For each goal, you've already identified the steps required to complete it. Beside each step, list one risk you'll need to take in order to achieve that step. Some action steps will have more risks than others; some will have none.

GOAL # 1	ACTION STEPS	RESOURCES	RISKS	PRIORITIES A-D
Goal # 1 Sail around the world	**Action Step 1:** Example: Find out how someone else did it.	I know someone who knows someone who sailed to Mexico. Contact him.	Leave my: career, income, security, home, identify	B-I can learn as I go
	Action Step 2: Buy a boat. Find the money.	Savings—use it Company—sell it—find a broker	Physical dangers, fear!	A-Can't go without boat
	Action Step 3: Find crew.	Start hanging out as sailing clubs, run ads.	Difficult to find someone I will like to join me.	B-Should have
	Action Step 4: Learn to navigate.	Take a class	Low risk to do, higher risk if I don't.	B-I can learn on the way

You can write your risks here:

_____

_____

_____

_____

Taking this one step further, for each risk, we're going to assess:

- Benefits
- Drawbacks
- Effects
- Results

Don't overcomplicate this. You're just trying to determine if you're willing to take the risks you've put on the list.

BENEFITS	DRAWBACKS	EFFECTS	RESULTS

_____

_____

_____

_____

Old habits die hard—especially if they are comfortable. But how important is it to hang onto them when they may be holding you back from your real purpose? Consider: How will your life be different if you do go for it 100 percent and use your goals to transform your vision into reality? I encourage you to be willing to take the risk—it's worth it.

CHAPTER 6

PERSONAL DECISION-MAKING

The number one question I'm asked is: How do you make the final decision to move forward? How do you take the first step? How did I make the enormous decision to take the ultimate risk and leave everything behind to sail around the world? I'm usually not asked about money, time, or skills, but how I made the decision to do it. For many, it's easy to see a broad picture and a big vision. It's not even that hard to make a plan. However, the difficulty occurs when faced with taking the first step in your plan. You have to make the decision and follow through on it.

In this chapter, you're going to discover how to make big decisions through prioritization. Do you have difficulty making decisions sometimes? Do you find it easier to make decisions in your professional life than for yourself? If something is wrong in your company, you work to remedy it immediately, right? Yet why do so many professionals not see a doctor when they feel something is wrong with their body?

Everybody faces decision-making challenges every day. You see a green light turn yellow—do you stop or run it? You make daily choices between vine ripe tomatoes and cherry tomatoes, between olive oil from Spain or from Italy, the cheap car wash or the works. "Should I buy those new shoes? They would look good on me, but they're expensive...Gee, I don't know." Sometimes you choose to buy the shoes, and sometimes you don't. And sometimes, you don't choose. "Ehhh, never mind, I'll think about it." Guess what, by making *no* decision, you just made a decision.

How did I make those decisions? This question can be answered in one word: *Priorities.*

You will start to get results right away by making decisions based on your priorities. "But Larry, wait, I don't know my personal priorities," you say. You don't? Okay, let's set your priorities.

Certainly, you use some sort of prioritization system in your professional life. It may not be identifiable as a system, but your brain does go through the process of prioritizing. Again, though, that's in your professional life. My experience shows that even though you may use a system of prioritization in your work life, you may not yet be using a system in your personal life.

Here's how I do it. I use the same system in my everyday personal life that we used on the boat. The original use of the system was to decide if we were ready to leave to go to sea. Were we ready to leave the dock and head out across a bay, a channel, or a three-thousand-mile ocean? Let me give you a simple example: If you're going to drive to Grandma's house and she lives a hundred miles away, and there are no gas stations along the way or in her small town, then what do you need before you leave? The answer is simple: enough gas for two hundred miles. That would be an "A" on the scale. So, it went like this onboard the yacht *Julia*:

> **A= Must have before going to sea**
> **B= Should have before going to sea**
> **C= Would be nice to have before going to sea**
> **D= Don't count on it, but hopefully someday we'll get to that**

So, for example, having a working engine was an 'A' or we couldn't even leave the marina. Varnishing the woodwork usually ended up in the 'D' category because nobody really liked to do that and it wasn't a critical priority.

Now take this easy system and incorporate it into your vision. When you know what your priorities are as you venture toward your dream, if you consistently make your decisions and choices based on those priorities, your decision-making process will be much easier and more consistent.

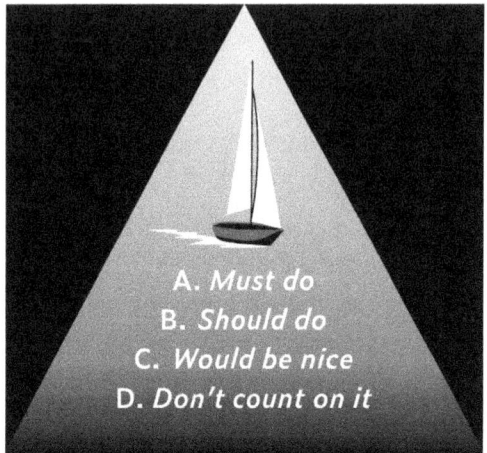

WHAT ARE YOUR PRIORITIES?

What are your priorities as you venture toward self-actualization? Are they to help people? To teach others? To make money? To help others and make money? To make your dream come true? Fulfill your fantasy of owning a winery? Castle-hop your way through Europe?

Which goal leading you to your vision is the 'A' goal, and which ones are the Bs, Cs, and Ds? Decide, because when you have your priorities in place, every following decision you make will become nearly automatic.

For example, my passion for sailing around the world was my 'A' priority. That meant everything below 'A' was to strengthen the possibility of that 'A' priority being achieved. Specifically and deliberately:

- I chose passion over fear. Yes, I was afraid, but my passion drove me to learn how to deal with my fears.

- I chose adventure over security. I knew I was leaving my security behind, but adventure was a higher priority.

- I chose spending my money on experiences rather than saving for the future. To me, the experience was a higher priority. I will admit that was an expensive decision, but it's one with which I'm still very happy.

Once you have your priorities in place, decisions about your vision and goals will come easy because you now have a system. Don't be fooled by its simplicity. And remember the more you use the system, the more subconscious and automatic to implement it will become.

ACTION GUIDE 6A: PRIORITIZING YOUR ACTION STEPS

Take a few moments to brainstorm your priorities. Then, referring back to the action steps you have previously identified in Action Guide 2, rate each action step according to its priority level using the ABCD system described in the last couple pages above.

1. List below your top priority goal.

   _____

   _____

   _____

   _____

   _____

2. Go back and take a look at the action steps you determined would need to be completed in order to achieve your first big goal. List them below.

   _____

   _____

   _____

   _____

   _____

3. Rate each action step based on priority, from A to D, with A being the highest priority and D being the lowest.

_____

_____

_____

_____

_____

_____

_____

4. Now look at your list above and decide which one, two, or three of your top-priority items you will complete—or get started on—this week or month.

_____

_____

_____

_____

_____

_____

_____

5. List below the action steps you have previously determined need to be completed in order to achieve your second big goal.

___

___

___

___

___

___

___

6. Rate each action step from A to D based on priority.

___

___

___

___

___

___

___

7. Rinse and repeat anytime you need to make a decision about moving forward or not. Pretty soon, this process will become second nature.

ACTION GUIDE 6B: DECISION TIME USING THE ABCD SYSTEM

Let's implement the ABCD Prioritization System in other areas of your life. Maybe you've been struggling with decisions that are *not* necessarily related to your big goals, but to something else in your life. Why not use the ABCD system and make those decisions now?

As an exercise, write down three issues on which you've been struggling to make a decision. These could be things that are not relevant to your encore. For example, one issue could be whether or not to buy a new car. If you don't have big decisions to make, try the system on little ones, such as what to have for lunch. What is your priority? Healthy, such as a salad, or taste, like a hamburger?

What are issues you want to try deciding with this system? Think about each pending decision, and determine your answer according to the ABCD system.

1. Record below the number one issue on which you've been struggling to make a decision lately.

    _____

    _____

    _____

2. Record another top issue on which you've been struggling to make a decision. Perhaps it's regarding your social life, taking up a hobby, or finally asking that new friend out on a date.

    _____

    _____

    _____

3. Record your third issue on which you've been struggling to make a decision.

_____

_____

_____

_____

Now, using your priority A–D system, make a decision on each of the above issues. What did you decide? Did you find it was easier to make a decision this way? Record your thoughts below.

_____

_____

_____

_____

As you venture toward your dream with your priorities in mind, while consistently making your decisions and choices based on those priorities, your decision-making process will become easier and more consistent. Keep practicing making decisions using your priorities as a guide until it becomes second nature. The more you practice, the easier it becomes. This will go a long way to helping you move toward your goals and your big vision. I hope you find the priority system ignites your willpower so you feel ready to implement your action steps, which will lead to the completion of your goals.

CHAPTER 7

MANAGING YOUR FEARS

If I were to ask you what the scariest moment in your life was, could you tell me? Take a moment to picture it in your mind. Perhaps it was learning to ride a bike as a child, an important job interview, or a tax audit. It could have been starting a new company, asking for someone's hand in marriage, or giving a speech to a large group. Even if this was the scariest moment in your life, most likely when you look back at that event, was it *'False Expectations Appearing Real'*? While this is often the case, sometimes the fear is truly real and you find yourself in a situation that is indeed frightening. And occasionally, an event is both: The fear is real, but the cause is overblown by our thoughts and imagination.

If you were to ask me the same question, the answer might surprise you. It wasn't dodging pirates in the Gulf of Aden, it wasn't being chased by Komodo dragons, and it wasn't even battling the worst storm of our lives in the middle of the Red Sea. My two-man crew and I had been caught in the exact wrong place at the wrong time in the Red Sea. A storm arrived a full day earlier than forecasted, and it turned out we had vastly underestimated its strength. Imagine our small boat flying off the top of a thirty-foot wave and slamming down into the trough below, shaking and shuddering like a cannon. The winds had come up quickly: First twenty knots, then thirty, forty, fifty, and when they hit sixty knots, I knew we were in trouble. The noise was deafening; the wind sounded like a wounded animal as it screamed through the rigging. It was cold, we were shivering, and we were pounding into the enormous seas. The waves were not only huge, but they were steep—steeper than I had ever seen, with breakers on their tops, and they were coming fast. I remember counting:

one thousand one, one thousand two, one thousand three, and *bam!* Another one would hit us. It was exhausting. We were drained after going at it for more than twenty-four hours. All I really wanted to do was go down below, crawl into a bunk, pull the covers up over my eyes, and wish it all away.

But then I looked at my crew, Ken and CJ, and saw their eyes were as wide as saucers. They were really scared. What about me, was I scared? I wouldn't use that word as I think terrified is more appropriate! You'd have to be crazy not to be scared in those conditions. The fear was definitely well-founded, and my imagination made it even worse. I was afraid for myself, for the boat, and most of all for my crew.

But fear—like all emotions—is contagious. I was the captain, the leader, and the last thing I needed was a crew frozen with fear. I needed my crew to do their jobs for the overall safety of the boat. I had to inspire confidence, motivation, and passion in them, and it didn't matter how rough it was. I didn't have any choice but to lead away from fear. But if I was so terrified, how did I get through my fears right then and lead fearlessly? I didn't. I was scared the entire duration of the storm, but I learned to use the fear to my advantage.

We all know that fear causes one of three reactions: fight, flight, or freeze. So I checked to see if there were any flights going out of the middle of the Red Sea that morning. Okay, not really, but it crossed my mind. Freezing to the point of inaction was not a possibility since it would have meant sure disaster. Our only choice was to stay and fight—and learn about fear. I learned a lot about fear that day. I learned:

- *Fear is Nature's way of making you focus on the task at hand.*
- *It sharpens your senses and makes you more alert.*
- *You can use fear to your advantage right then and there.*

In this chapter, you're going to learn how to use fear to your advantage. It's natural to be afraid when stepping out of your comfort zone as you work toward your goals. For example, you might fear:

- Giving up the good—for a chance at the great.
- Having to step out of certain elements of your comfort zone.
- Going down the wrong path in your choices.
- The risk might not be worth the reward.

Your mind can easily take you to places of fear rather than inspiration if you let it. We are all motivated twice as much to move *away* from that which we fear as we are to move *toward* what we want. Consequently, it's no surprise that fear often rules the day.

TWO STEPS TO MANAGING YOUR FEAR

That all changes for you from this moment on, because any fears you may have about taking your next big step toward your encore are no longer in charge. From now forward, you will use fear to your advantage. It's not all that difficult. There are only two steps to learning to use fear to your advantage.

The first step is to recognize you are afraid. You've felt and seen fear. If you had been with us that day in the Red Sea, you would have seen my palms sweating, my eyes wide and darting all around, and my muscles all pumped up, and you could have heard my heart beating through my chest from three feet away. Does any of this sound familiar? Think back to your scary moment, and you'll remember similar signs.

When you recall how to recognize the fear, you may also remember how it brought everything into focus, sharpened your senses, and made you more alert. This is nature's way of arming you with higher than normal senses for fight or flight. When I was at the wheel in thirty-foot seas, you better believe I was focused, sharp, and alert. And while I was still afraid, I was a better performer. This naturally occurring phenomenon is indeed a gift. When it arrives, recognize it.

The second step in using fear to your advantage is a little bit trickier. You must accept and embrace that you're afraid. Yes, you read that correctly: Accept and even embrace fear. By taking this important step, you disarm the fear. You take away its power when you say to yourself: "Okay, I'm afraid. Now, instead of running away, since I know the benefits fear can give me, I'm going to let it in." Then you can embrace what the fear is doing *for* you. It's making you sharper, focused, and more alert. You can use those newfound powers to your advantage right there in that moment.

Fear is like that little red devil that sits on your shoulder: the bad guy who tells you to have that third cocktail or that fourth cookie. When you recognize and embrace fear, it's like saying to your fears, *'You can come along for the ride, but you no longer have any say in what I feel or how I act. I know you're there, and I know you're trying to do bad things, but I know better. Larry told me you could do good things for me. So there! You're not the boss of me, and you no longer rule the day.'* Don't listen to the wind as it howls through the rigging trying to scare you. Get behind the wheel and start steering.

Can you believe dragons, pirates, and storms were *not* the scariest moments of my life?

Then what could it possibly have been? That moment was reserved for a cold crisp morning in December, when I sailed out beneath the Golden Gate Bridge, turned south, and headed for places unknown. The emotional upheaval I felt that day was far more fearful than any physical terror I faced. And that was the day I learned to face fear, which I went on to do nearly every day for the next six years. Fear and risk became the norm.

YOUR FEARS: ARE THEY LOGICAL?

Fear is emotional, and often the expectations of that fear are exaggerated and create false evidence in our minds. Here, logic is the hero of the day because logic is grounded in facts. By applying logic to your fears, you can then see most of the fears are "False Expectations (or Evidence) Appearing Real."

Here is an example of how I managed my fear of making a major ocean voyage. Read it to help you get clear about one of your fears in connection to something you want to actualize in your future. For my fear of crossing big oceans, I determined these were the three elements that made up this fear:

1. *Losing sight of land, getting lost*

2. *Big storms in the middle of the ocean that might sink us*

3. *Running out of food*

Next, I did a little brainstorming to provide logical answers to those fears.

1. *Losing sight of land: It is actually safer at sea than near shore. A not-so-famous sailor named Jacobson once said, "It's not the ocean that gets you, it's the hard bits around the edges." Most boats get into trouble when they are close to land, not at sea. Modern GPS navigation systems make it difficult to get lost at sea.*

2. *Big storms in the middle of the ocean: Most of the time, you can see storms coming on satellite weather pictures. Preparation and training with my crew on what actions to take during bad weather helped me manage my fears.*

3. *Running out of food: We stocked the boat with two months' worth of food, and we also caught lots of fish.*

Now it's time for you to try it. Refer to the Action Guide, then write down one fear you have about realizing your dream:

What are three elements that form the basis of this fear for you?

Let's take this one step further and apply these same techniques to fears related to *you* achieving *your* goals. Refer to the next section in the Action Guide and envision and *anticipate* potential fears relating to every step you'll be taking. Now see yourself accepting those fears, being okay with them, and living with them.

FEAR ISN'T SO BAD

You now know that it's okay to be afraid because fear can be your ally. It can work to your advantage, especially if you *anticipate fear* before it happens. By previewing your imagined fears before they actually happen, you get to examine the fear and see logically it's probably filling you with False Expectations Appearing Real.

And always keep this in your back pocket: *Passion Trumps Fear*, the subject of my first TEDx talk. You can watch that talk on my website at: www.LarryJacobson.com/speaker. Your passion will drive you through any obstacle that stands in your way. Always know you can rely on your passion to keep you moving forward.

Now that you know how to use fear to your advantage, here's where you're going to use it in taking your next step beyond your work career. To make your vision a reality and achieve the goals in your plan, you will have to:

- Recognize and embrace your fear of leaving the old and familiar. As someone who has advanced through your career, you have likely mastered a skill or two. You have honed your craft, you understand the challenges, and you are used to having answers to problems that arise every day. You're not afraid of anything that's thrown your way in your current role as it's all quite familiar. You are now preparing yourself because you know that's going to change to the unfamiliar as new situations arise in your life's next act.

- Rise above the fear of what the new might be. New experiences are coming your way, potentially including problems you've not dealt with before, such as learning new skills and being a beginner again at something. These can cause fear to come up for you. But you have been there before. You have the ability, it's just a different story.

- Make a plan. This will be a new plan, one you have never written before, and you may have to modify it as you go. No problem. Besides, with a plan, at least you have something to change.

- Identify and follow through on the first step in that plan. Just before taking the first step in your plan, you're going to feel butterflies. You're metaphorically about to step off the curb, to dive into the pool, to jump out of the airplane (with a parachute, hopefully). Of course you're going to be afraid, but now you will embrace that fear.

Remember what Paulo Coelho said in *The Alchemist*: *"Once you want something, all the universe conspires to help you achieve it."* All you have to do is take that first step. The joy is in the journey. Trying new things, learning new skills, and doing new activities will add excitement to your life and re-energize you.

ACTION GUIDE 7A: WHAT ARE YOU AFRAID OF?

In this exercise, you're going to identify one of your biggest fears about moving forward with your goals and vision. After examining it closely, there's a good chance you'll see this fear as False Expectations Appearing Real. And even if it is a well-founded fear, you'll know how to manage it. You can follow this same exercise for as many fears as you like. The important part here is to learn and apply the process.

1. What is a big fear weighing on you?

   _____

   _____

   _____

   _____

   _____

2. Examine the fear closely; what are three elements that cause you to feel this fear?

   _____

   _____

   _____

   _____

   _____

3. What are the pragmatic counterarguments to the three elements above? That is, what are the logical explanations of why these reasons aren't so valid?

_____

_____

_____

_____

4. Identify how these fears help you. For example, if you're planning a long canoe trip and are afraid of drowning, now you'll buy a good life vest. Or if you're afraid of not being strong enough for the trip, that's okay! Get your physical checkup, then join a gym to get stronger so you'll feel confident and ready.

_____

_____

_____

_____

5. What will you tell yourself and how will you act the next time this fear raises its ugly head?

_____

_____

_____

_____

ACTION GUIDE 7B: ANTICIPATE YOUR FEAR

By previewing your imagined fears before they actually happen, you can examine them and realize they are filling you with False Expectations Appearing Real. So, let's have a look ahead at your potential fears.

1. What is one fear you are expecting to face, even one you may not have thought of yet? By identifying it now, you won't be surprised when it shows up.

   _____

   _____

   _____

   _____

   _____

2. You can follow this same exercise for as many expected fears as you like. The important part here is to learn the process. List some other fears you can expect.

   _____

   _____

   _____

   _____

   _____

3. Additionally, to make your vision a reality and achieve the goals in your plan, you'll need to overcome the fear of leaving the old and the familiar. What is it you're afraid of leaving behind?

_____

_____

_____

_____

_____

_____

_____

4. Have confidence you will rise above the fear of what the new might bring. Beginning something new and unfamiliar can be scary. Jot down something that will be part of your plan—something you don't know how to do yet. Remember, the joy is in the journey and the learning.

_____

_____

_____

_____

_____

_____

_____

5. You're going to be making a new plan—one you've never written before—and this can be scary. Are you afraid of writing this plan? Why? You've written plans before, and you can write this one too.

_____
_____
_____
_____
_____
_____

6. Without action, a plan is just a piece of paper. Once you begin taking action, the rest will follow. Can you identify the first step in your plan? When will you take that first step?

_____
_____
_____
_____
_____
_____

CHAPTER 8

FINDING AND KEEPING A POSITIVE PERSPECTIVE

In this chapter, you're going to learn how your *view* of challenging circumstances and events is directly related to your ability to persevere through them.

Circumstances and events happen. There's often not much we can do to change or redirect them after they have occurred. If you've been in control your entire life, it's difficult to let go of being in charge, and that trait will be tested as you move forward toward your goals. In Chapter 4, I wrote about giving up my identity to go sailing. And in Chapter 5, I described how when I returned, I found myself in hotels where I used to have clout but was now just an average hotel guest with no influence on operations. That's when I coined the phrase, "Do you know who I used to be?" And guess what, things were just fine without my influence on the hotel's operations. I just needed an attitude adjustment to allow things to be as they are and accept them.

> The good news is you can control your perspective about the circumstances and events happening in your life. You get to choose how you feel and how you react to any given circumstance or event. What outlook will you choose?

While sailing, I learned the difference between a good passage and a bad one was not weather or mechanical breakdowns, but rather my perspective. It's your outlook that matters; the way you view and react to the inevitable circumstances and events that happen to you. I will be the first to admit learning to have a positive perspective is a process, not an event. At the beginning of my journey around the world, I was pretty shaken up when something broke. I had little mechanical experience and didn't know how we would repair those breakdowns. Could they be fixed? Some repairs required only our own skills, some required friends, some required genuine mechanics, some required radio calls via single-side-band radio to a mechanic on shore, some required new parts, and all required more time than expected. But over time I learned that one way or another, almost everything was fixable. And by the end of the trip six years later, I took just about anything in stride.

One night during one of the last legs of our voyage, when we lost our alternator motoring up the coast of California, I started laughing! What was I going to do, cry? There's no crying in sailing. Besides, laughing is so much more fun. And since we had a spare alternator, we simply installed it at sea because installing an alternator was elementary to us by then.

When you have a positive perspective, and learn to accept what is happening, your view of the world changes. You might have to climb up the mast to fix something while at sea, and you go up with a frown, angry that the wind vane needs fixing. However, while you're up there hanging on for dear life as you make the repair, you take a quick glance around and notice the view, which is incredible. Then, you think about your perspective—from the top of the mast of your own boat sailing across an ocean. And you get a feeling like no other that makes it all worth it, and you come down the mast smiling. How you view what happens in your life is empowering in either a positive or negative manner. *Choose the positive.*

Sometimes your hand is forced and you have no choice about what comes your way. It's not a matter of choice, just acceptance. Sailing through the Caribbean on our way to the Panama Canal, we had considered stopping in Cartagena, Colombia. But we had a scheduled date for going through the Canal, and were running short on time. Plus, there were rumors of pirates in the local waters, soldiers on the streets, and drug war violence, so we set our course directly for Panama. By this time in the odyssey,

I had become expert at reading weather maps, so it wasn't as though I didn't expect the rough conditions we encountered: fifteen-foot seas and thirty to thirty-five knot winds. We had been in much worse, we were used to it, and we were sailing downwind, surfing the swells and having fun.

My friend Nick, an accomplished sailor, was at the helm when all of a sudden we heard a loud *"bang!"* By this time, we *knew* loud noises are not a good sign on boats. The next thing we knew, the steering went loose, and Nick had almost no control of the rudder.

He summed it up nicely when he said, 'Uh-oh.' He was turning the wheel wildly, steering the boat like an old Cadillac to prevent broaching, which means the boat turning sideways to the waves. I made my way down to the bilge to take a look at the steering quadrant and saw the problem. The steering cable had ripped one of the pulleys off of its mount, and there was now too much play in the cable for it to be effective. The wheel was essentially useless. However, the autopilot came to the rescue because it bypassed the steering cables.

We altered course and immediately headed for Cartagena, about a day's sail away. Schedule or not, pirates or not, soldiers or not, we were headed for Cartagena. We felt quite vulnerable.

We ended up loving Cartagena. There were no pirates, our steering gear was fixed in a day by a marine engineer as competent as any we'd met, and we were warmly welcomed by locals; the soldiers on street corners gave tourist directions, the food was fantastic and inexpensive, and the city turned out to be one of the most beautiful in the world. It was all just the way we looked at it. It was all our perspective. It was a classic case of making lemonade out of lemons.

Through the changes you are about to make in your life, look at it all with a positive perspective. It's easy to see the bad in things. Anybody can do that. But if you look a little harder, if you look with a positive perspective, you can find the good in just about anything. Hey, Ship Happens. What are you going to do, cry?

Why is keeping a positive perspective so important to what you're learning here? The answer is your attitude or perspective will affect your ability to persevere in your new arena. In taking your next big step beyond your career, chances are you will be in unfamiliar waters. You will meet with setbacks and discouragement. Recognize them as par for the course, and don't let them stop you in your quest. How do you do this? How do you continually look at the world with a positive perspective? The answer is practice.

Most of our negative reactions get us nowhere and are too often the beginning of a downward spiral. The negative jumps out and discourages us from wanting to press on. The media likes the negative. If I had died or my boat had sunk on my trip around the world, I'd be famous. But because I did things right and made it home safely, my journey around the world was a nonstory because there's no drama in a happy tale.

Looking at events and circumstances with a positive perspective requires practice, and that's what I'd like you to begin doing. Consciously observe one event, circumstance, or person that elicits a negative reaction in you. At the very moment when you feel your blood starting to boil, notice your negative reaction to what you're seeing and acknowledge that you are having a negative reaction. You did this before when you learned to acknowledge fear. Once you have recognized the negative reaction you're having, then you can step away and see the feeling as something separate from you.

> Right there, on the spot, picture yourself reaching out and flipping a switch that changes your reaction from negative to positive.

FLIP THE SWITCH

Choose to change your reaction to a positive one. *Choose* to find the good and focus only on that. Hold that positive perspective and let go of the negative. Remember, the event happened anyway. There's nothing you can do about it, so you may as well smile, laugh about it, and not let it bring you down. *It is a choice*. That's the only difference between seeing the good and the bad. It's *your* choice, so choose to have a positive perspective. Seeing things in a positive manner motivates you to keep going in any pursuit.

You have to practice this, so start with simple things. For example, you walk into the bank and there's a long line. Your initial reaction is negative. Change it by looking at the possibility of striking up a conversation with the person in front of you in line. Can you flip the switch?

You get a flat tire, so you take your car into the tire dealer for a repair or a new tire, and of course you're not happy about it. While doing a routine inspection, the mechanic notices your brake pads are so worn that they would have failed in a real emergency stop. Of course you replace them, but you're not happy about that, either. That's the negative perspective. The positive perspective is that flat tire probably saved your life when you needed to slam on the brakes the following day. Anybody can see the negative. That's easy to do. You have to dig deeper to find the good, but it's there. It's always there.

In your Action Guide, record three of these events in which you changed your perspective. You'll want to keep these so you have visible evidence to remind you that you have the ability to flip the switch.

Congratulations! You've learned how to change your perspective. Do you feel confident in your ability to adopt a positive outlook as you move toward your goal?

ACTION GUIDE 8: KEEPING A POSITIVE PERSPECTIVE

In this exercise, we'll explore how you can make small shifts in your attitude or perspective about events and circumstances. These changes in how you view things will strengthen your tenacity in pursuit of your goals.

1. List below three events in which you changed your perspective, and as a result, were able to stay positive and perhaps even enjoy the situation you were in. Keep these handy to remind yourself you have the ability to *flip your attitude switch.*

   _____

   _____

   _____

   _____

   _____

2. Take one of the above instances in which you were able to change your perspective from negative to positive. How did you do it? How did it make you feel?

   _____

   _____

   _____

   _____

   _____

3. Think of another instance—perhaps a time when you thought all hell was breaking loose—where you were able to change your perspective from negative to positive. How did you do it? How did it make you feel?

_____

_____

_____

_____

_____

_____

_____

You have always known circumstances and events can happen without your being able to control them. And often there's not much you can do to change or direct their unfolding after they have occurred.

However, you have now learned there is something you can control: your *perspective* about events and circumstances. *You get to choose* how you feel, how you react, and what outlook or attitude you will adopt moving forward. Remember that choosing is the key. You can choose what attitude to have in the moment and how you react to your surroundings. And yes, sometimes that choice has to start with acceptance.

Keeping a positive perspective will affect your ability to persevere in your new direction. In taking your next big step beyond your professional career, you may encounter setbacks and discouragement. Don't let them stop your quest. Remember you can *flip the switch* of your attitude from negative to positive. More often than not, it's up to you—it's your choice.

In the next chapter, we're going to examine perseverance and the ability to stick with your dream until you succeed. It's your positive perspective that will provide this perseverance.

CHAPTER 9
PERSEVERANCE—STICKING WITH IT

Do you know the three skills it takes to get a boat around the world? They are bravery, perseverance, and the ability to open a bottle of wine without a corkscrew. Bravery is found out there at sea: you either become brave or you turn around. Opening the wine is easy; you can find that on YouTube. The reason so few people make it all the way around the world is it takes an enormous amount of perseverance. It takes tenacity to withstand the mechanical breakdowns, weather setbacks, and emotional highs and lows of sailing.

You have tenacity. You have advanced through your career, so it's already proven you have the perseverance to stick with something until you succeed. You developed comfort with your professional life, and you knew what it took to get the job done. Now that you're going to embark on a new venture, you may experience doubts that are foreign to you. Perhaps you're not an expert yet, but remember:

> *Your passion for what you are about to embark upon will drive you through the challenges and obstacles along the way. Your positive perspective is what will provide the perseverance you will need to succeed.*

I know this from experience. I came 'this close' to turning around along the way. So many times, I thought it would have been so much easier to just throw in the towel. But I didn't really have any choice because my passion wouldn't let go of me...so I kept going. And my positive perspective, the way I saw all of these roadblocks, reinforced my thinking that success was possible.

There were plenty of challenges that tried to derail me from completing my journey. We lost our autopilot multiple times, we had to rebuild our engine, we nearly lost our mast in a storm on our way to Australia, and there were more mechanical failures than I can recall.

And we had emotional breakdowns. We faced and overcame challenges each and every day for six years. That's a long time, and it took an enormous amount of effort to persevere and stay the distance. None of these things stopped me. My passion for my dream and my positive perspective kept me going, just as *your* positive attitude will keep you sticking with yours.

We all have a great deal of strength and tenacity within us. It makes itself available to us when we *need* it, such as when faced with Komodo dragons, real live pirates, and big storms. But this ability to persevere is also available to us when we *want* it. We just have to dig for it. And that takes practice.

Just like working on keeping a positive attitude, perseverance is a skill best learned from practice. I found myself thrust onto the stage not knowing my lines many times while sailing around the world. Every day there was something new I had to figure out for the first time. Sometimes I missed being back in business because of how comfortable I had been in that life; sailing around the world was uncomfortable because of the enormity of the challenges. *It took a while for me to learn that the challenges that shook me out of my comfort zone made me feel alive again.* I am sharing my wide-ranging emotions with you because I want you to expect similar ups and downs as you pursue your dream. Unexpected and unbearable circumstances are difficult to deal with at best. However, they are easier to deal with when you expect them.

It's easy to persevere under good conditions. Anybody can do that. That's not tenacity, that's just going with the flow. In tough times, though, it helps to have had practice so you can succeed in persevering through criticism, through your learning curve, and through the setbacks you will encounter along the way.

You also must recognize when you're in a situation that requires perseverance. When you see you're going to be in it for the long haul, that makes it real. Once you recognize how real it is, you can find the subconscious drive to dig deep for the strength you need to get through that situation.

ACTION GUIDE 9A: PERSEVERANCE—STICKING WITH IT

In your Action Guide, examine your goals and the action steps needed for those goals. Predict a situation that will require perseverance on your road to fulfilling your ambitions. Then, beside each situation, write one or more ideas that will help you to stay the course.

Now, next to those same situations, write about the rewards you will gain if you persevere and overcome each particular obstacle. What about failure, what would that look like?

For example, what required the most tenacity while sailing was making it through the mechanical breakdowns that happened so frequently. I knew that was going to be a challenge, and I expected it would require perseverance. One of the ideas I came up with to help me persevere was to stock every spare part imaginable for every system onboard. The rewards for doing so came almost daily as those spare parts were used to fix something. I became a parts hoarder, and it paid off handsomely.

Using that example as a model, record your thoughts in the Action Guide.

PREDICT A SITUATION THAT WILL REQUIRE PERSEVERANCE	BRAINSTORM IDEAS TO HELP YOU STAY THE COURSE	WHAT DOES FAILURE LOOK LIKE?	IDENTIFY THE REWARDS OF PERSEVERING

As you examine your action steps, predict a situation that will require perseverance on the road to fulfilling your ambition. Then you'll identify ideas to stay the course, rewards for persevering, and the consequences of failure.

1. Predict a situation that will require perseverance.

_____

_____

_____

_____

_____

_____

_____

2. Brainstorm ideas to help you stay the course.

___

3. What does failure look like?

___

4. Identify the rewards of persevering.

ACTION GUIDE 9B: INTUITIVE BENEFITS ANALYSIS

Take a few moments to think about your potential outcomes as you move forward.

1. How will your life be different if you *don't* take action and do not achieve the goals you set in this book?

___

2. How will your life be different if you *do* take action and achieve the goals you set?

_____

_____

_____

_____

_____

_____

_____

_____

My challenge to you is to commit to practicing *perseverance*—keep moving toward your goals, overcoming each obstacle and fear as they arise. I know you can do it.

In this chapter, you discovered that there is an enormous amount of strength and tenacity inside of you available when you need it most, when faced with emergency or dangerous situations.

You also have this ability to persevere under normal circumstances. You just have to dig for it, and that takes practice. Are you practicing persevering in your goals that will lead to your vision becoming a reality? Have you examined where you think you'll need tenacity the most in reaching your goals? When you're aware of the need, it's easier to take action and persevere.

You're approaching the end of the book. In the next chapter, you'll commit to everything you've been learning, creating, and dreaming about during this journey. Your commitment will be critical in achieving your goals. Whether your vision is big or small, it still requires commitment from you.

CHAPTER 10

COMMITMENT TO YOUR PLAN OF ACTION

You have been a success in your professional career. You are an achiever, or you wouldn't have made it this far. I understand very well how hard it can be to think of letting go of that achievement and identity.

It's worth the risk. Depending on what you came up with in your risk analysis, chances are you've realized you're going to have to risk something to create a new identity, even if it's only your past identity. There will be criticism, false starts, wrong directions, and financial costs, and more than once you will ask yourself, "What have I done?" Yes, you have passion for something. You have a vision. But is it worth the risk? Is it logical? Does it really matter if you make this change in your life? Remind yourself that you're here, working through this book, because you're committed to making a change—and it's worth it. One helpful way of committing to your new self is to change what you say about yourself.

> Eliminate from your vocabulary, "I'm a retired..." When someone asks what you do for a living, say, "I'm a..." and insert your new passion and goals. If you're still working on defining who you are, say, "I'm working on my ideal next phase for my life and making my dreams come true."

"Is it logical, is it worth it, and does it matter if I make this change in my life?" I asked myself those same questions after twenty years in the corporate world. I'd collected expensive suits and watches, built a solid reputation, and amassed a client list of distinction. All was going along fine until I woke up one day and faced the fact that I was burnt out and wasn't looking forward to each day. It wasn't that there was no enjoyment anymore, but rather realizing how fast my life was flying by. Even though I had the greatest career I could imagine at the time, I felt stuck, as if I would be doing the same thing forever.

I questioned my purpose in life, the satisfaction I was receiving, and the contribution I was making. I wondered how much of what I was doing mattered to the world. And there was this voice that kept popping up more and more often, an inner voice reminding me of my dream of sailing around the world. I was having a midlife crisis.

A midlife crisis is when you reach the top rung of the ladder and realize you've leaned it up against the wrong wall. You have to climb down, move the ladder to a new wall, and start climbing again. The good part is you already know how to climb, and this time, it will have a different purpose.

It's never too late to be who you could have been.

So, in answer to the question, Is it worth the risk? Oh yes, is it ever. I wouldn't change what I chose for all the money in the world. That's how confident I am in the decisions I made, and I never would have known if I hadn't taken the first step of my plan.

You've worked your entire life at your profession. Your left brain is so overworked it's probably taken over. But you don't die happy having satisfied your left brain, you die happy having achieved a life of meaning. *Why not let your heart and emotional desires lead for a change?*

Even if you're happy in your career, there are things in this world more meaningful than making money. You're taking a risk because something bigger and more important is calling you. If you're afraid of letting go of your identity, all the more reason to take the risk. Otherwise, how will you ever know what else is possible?

THE SELF-ACTUALIZED YOU

Someone who seeks self-actualization on Maslow's hierarchy of needs is likely to match the following description: You trust your own judgment and are not susceptible to social pressures, you're compassionate to others and to yourself. You can laugh at yourself; you're spontaneous, curious, and creative, and you seek peak experiences that leave a lasting impression. Have you achieved nearly everything you set out to do in your life? Most likely you have, but you've realized there is more for you to experience.

These characteristics are within *you*. Now it's time to commit.

As you think about your encore, you may have decided to do something either to better your local community or to fulfill an aspiration you've always dreamed of for yourself. You may have discovered what you want to do, or you may not yet know what that is. What I hope you have concluded is that it's time to do something different. Life is short, and as far as I know, we only get one chance at this amazing opportunity called living. Live your life not with the glass half empty, not even with the glass full, but let the glass overflow and pour out onto the table.

To grow emotionally and intellectually, we must continually feed our minds with knowledge. Without new and invigorating food for the brain, we remain stagnant. If you needed permission from yourself to grow, to change, or take a new journey in a different direction, you now have it. You have now gone through the process of approving your own future growth. You have hopefully identified what you want to do, analyzed the steps involved, and set goals. You've considered the risks, made tough decisions, and worked through your fears, and you now have a positive perspective on moving into your next step in life. I'd say you have earned your permission.

Now it's time to commit and solidify your deepest conviction that not only are you going to do this, but you are going to stick with it and follow through. Your definition of success will be different than in your previous work life, of course. For example, if creating art is what you want to do now, then you will have succeeded when your first piece of art is finished. Then you can build upon that success.

I COMMIT

In your Action Guide at the end of this chapter, there's a space for you to write your commitment statement. It should start with, "I commit to…" and then you will fill in your big dream that is going to be your next step beyond your career. Write it down.

Commit to staying the course. I understand you may drift off course here and there, but be aware that even a small change of course can affect where you end up. If you were to set sail from Mexico across the Pacific Ocean to the Marquesas Islands, you would be sailing approximately 2,750 miles. If you cross that distance with a compass error of just one degree, you will miss the island by nearly fifty miles. If your compass error is five degrees, you'll miss the island by 250 miles.

Hold your course and stick with your plan by following the steps you have created in your Action Guide. Use the knowledge you have gained in this book about who you are, and you will make it across *your* ocean and arrive at your intended destination.

As you moved through this book, you have identified your big dream, written your vision statement, broken your vision statement down into reasonable and achievable goals, conducted a SWOT analysis, identified the risks and the resources required to overcome them, learned how to make sound decisions through prioritization, learned how to use fear to your advantage, and seen the rewards associated with a positive attitude and perseverance.

Each step of the way, you have recorded thoughts and strategies in your Action Guide. Now your Action Guide will serve as a comprehensive plan to keep you on course—use it as a reference as you are approaching obstacles or looking for next steps. Review each section. Do you agree with your original responses? Would you change or add to them? Take some time to do that now so the Action Guide will best serve you on your path to fulfilling your dream. Here is a quick review chapter by chapter.

1. First of all, look at your Big Dream and review the details. Is there anything new you want to add? Is this still the encore you want? Are there more details you can add? If you like your encore and the vision is clear, then move on. If not, then write a new one. Now you know how to do that.

2. Next, look at your goals and find those with the "A" priority. What is the first action step listed for each? Assess the potential risk, the resources needed, and the priority. If it's still an "A," then begin with that *first action step*.

3. Review your *SWOT analysis*. By now, some of these elements may have shifted from one category to another. For example, a weakness may have been addressed, or perhaps it was a fear and that fear is gone.

4. Now take a close look at your *risk analysis*. As you review each of the risks you identified with each action step, think them through again. After knowing what you know now, is each one still a viable risk? Chances are that your increased confidence eliminates some elements from being risky.

5. The next section of the Action Guide is where you practiced making decisions. At the beginning of the book, it didn't matter if the decisions were big or small, or even all that important. Now I suggest you make bigger decisions and make them about your *next step*. Even if it's just one decision, like "Yes, I'm going to do this!" You've experienced making many decisions in the course of your working life. However, we all get out of practice, and the more you practice making decisions using the ABCD priority system, the more naturally the decisions will come to you. Try it for three days again. Make decisions and note when you're using the system. The more you do this, the more implementing your priorities will sink in and become habit.

6. When you addressed fear, you wrote down something you were afraid of doing, seeing, or experiencing. Then you asked why you were afraid of this and provided the logical solution to those fears. And you went on to learn to use those fears to your advantage. On this go-round, I recommend you put your Big Dream as your fear. Even if you're not afraid of taking your next big step in life, put it in this section. Write why you are or were afraid of taking this step, and then brainstorm the solution to those fears. This is going to solidify your embracing your fears about your encore, and then you'll be ready to move forward. If you are still hesitating to take your next step because of fear, reread how to manage your fears, recognizing that most likely they are False Expectations Appearing Real.

7. You recorded three events in which you changed your perspective. Are they little or big events? Now I suggest you do this with three even bigger events. For example, instead of the usual line in the bank, the bank was closed. Your card didn't work in the ATM, and you can't figure out why. You're out of cash in a strange town where you don't know anybody, your car has broken down, and the mechanic will only release your car to you with cash. Change your perspective on something like that from your own life, and record it in the Action Guide for you to look back on. If you can go from a negative perspective to a positive one in that scenario, I'd say you're ready. And that was an easy one because obviously you get to know the mechanic and his family, they invite you to stay at their house until the bank opens in the morning, and you all become lifelong friends.

_____

_____

_____

_____

_____

_____

_____

_____

_____

_____

_____

8. Review the perseverance you will need for each action step you wrote in your Action Guide. Does it still seem so daunting? Seem more possible? If not, brainstorm some additional ideas that will help motivate you and keep you focused. Having a strategy to keep yourself on track, stay positive, and proactively respond to change will help you as you stay the course through uncharted waters.

_____

_____

_____

_____

_____

_____

_____

_____

_____

_____

_____

_____

_____

9. And lastly, review your commitment statement. Does it sit well with you? Do you like it? There's nobody else here for you to please, so you should love it, and if you don't, then rewrite it.

We started out with visioning your big picture. By completing this book, you now have the smaller steps necessary to make your vision a reality. Step by step, you can make your life's encore happen. And while you're taking these steps, keep your vision in your mind. Ask yourself these questions again:

- What is it in life that I really want?

- What really makes me happy and gives me satisfaction?

- What cause, passion, or purpose will keep me going through the storms and rough seas?

- When I'm on my last breaths, what is it I will say I'm glad I did?

- Or what is it I'll say I wish I had done?

- What do I want to create?

- What do I want to contribute?

- What do I want people to say about me after I'm gone?

- What kind of person do I want the world to see me as being?

- I know the steps I need to take. When will I take the first step?

Congratulations—you persevered and are well on your way to finding your encore. By completing this book, you have proven your dedication and commitment to creating an encore filled with purpose and fulfillment. Now, when you show the same commitment to your goals and to following your Action Steps, you will achieve your vision. You have what it takes.

You have a vision, you've set goals, made tough decisions, and worked through your fears, and you've created a positive perspective about your next steps in life. You know there will be risks associated with your plan, and you've analyzed your priorities. In fact, you may have noticed you analyzed every step along the way of creating your new plan of action. I'm pretty sure by now you're itching for someone to ask, "Have you thought this through?" And now you can say with 100 percent confidence you most certainly have!

You've had enough left-brain planning for now. It's time to let your emotional right brain take over and do what feels good. You are well on your way to achieving self-actualization and will be one of the few who actually get there, not just talk about it. Abraham Maslow would be proud of you, and so am I.

Now for your final exercise, you'll put it all together and create your plan of action.

CHAPTER 11

YOUR ENCORE PLAN

To create your encore plan, write a few lines responding to the following prompts:

1. This is my *vision*, dream, and the direction I'd like for my encore.

_____

_____

_____

_____

_____

_____

_____

_____

2. My *goals* and *action steps* are in order of priority.

GOALS	ACTION STEPS	PRIORITY	NOTES

3. These are my main strengths and opportunities. I will capitalize on them to help achieve my goals as well as ultimately my vision.

4. My weaknesses and threats are here, along with any "buts."

5. Here are *risks* I might be taking along with their potential *benefits*, *drawbacks*, *effects*, and *results*.

_____

_____

_____

_____

_____

_____

_____

_____

_____

_____

_____

_____

_____

_____

_____

_____

_____

6. This is my biggest fear about moving forward toward my goals and my dream.

7. Here is my biggest challenge to persevering, where I feel I'll need the most tenacity.

8. How committed am I? Here's what I'll need to commit to in order to make this plan succeed.

9. Here are my first steps. I will take the first step today because I remember what Paulo Coelho said in *The Alchemist*: *"When you want something, all the universe conspires to help you achieve it."*

_____

_____

_____

_____

_____

_____

_____

_____

_____

_____

_____

_____

_____

You now have a plan. When will you take your first step?

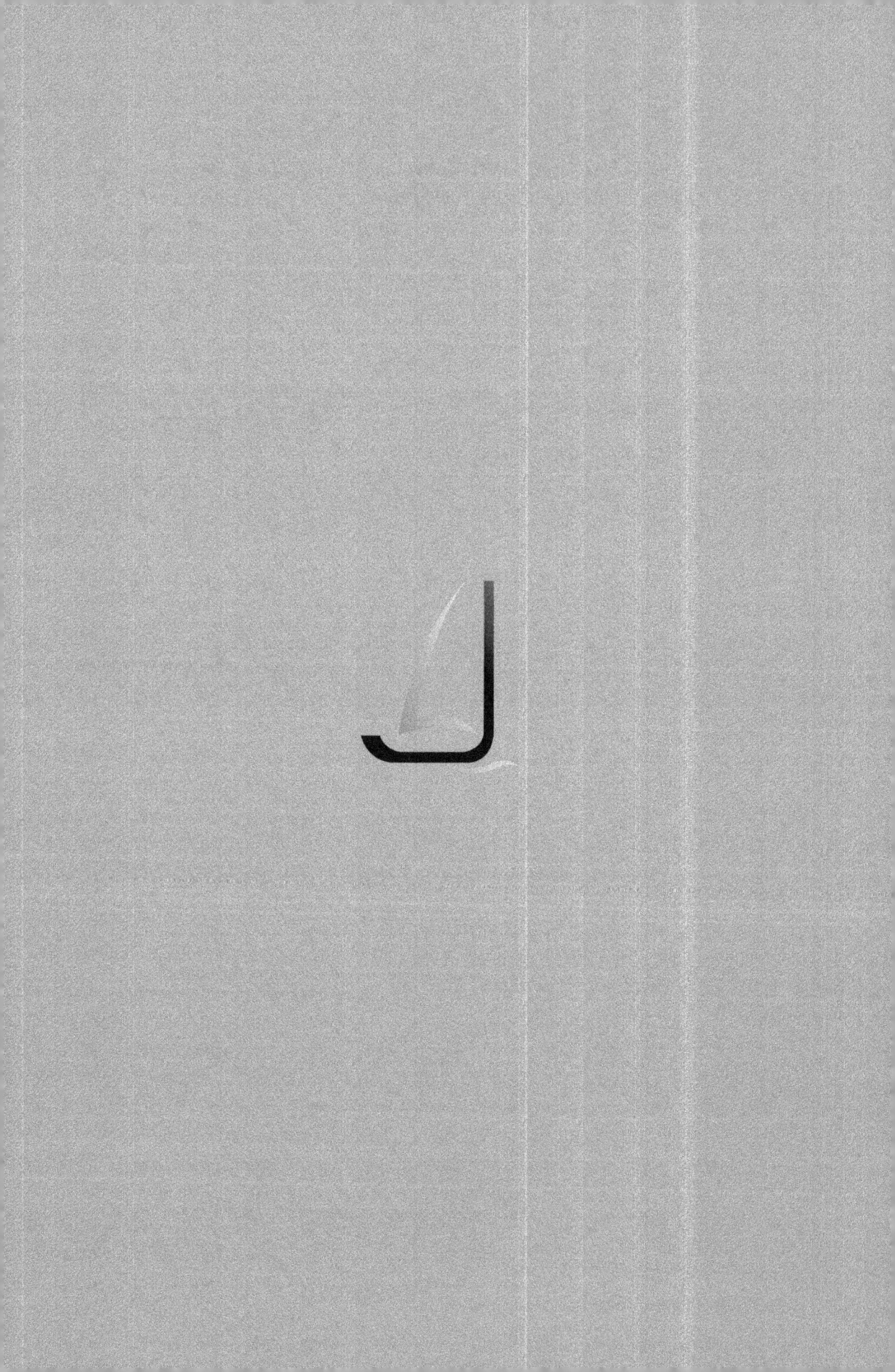

BONUS CHAPTER 12

BEGIN WITH THE END

I have fielded many questions about transitions, how they work, and if there is an actual process. I have added this bonus chapter to share more about the transition process you will be following to discover your new identity. Unless you are going to continue in the same profession until your last breath, you are going to go through this reinvention, transition, and discovery process. Some, like me, will go through it multiple times in their life.

For the most part, we aren't terribly conscious of the process because we are so busy doing the process. I recommend being aware and conscious about the transition process, which means knowing how these transitions happen. I agree with the work of the late William Bridges, who developed this theory, one which is widely accepted as gospel on the subject of transitions.

THERE ARE THREE PHASES TO TRANSITION

1. *All transitions begin with an end.* Yes, I know it sounds counterintuitive, but it's true. Think about these and other events, and you can see they are actually the end of something.

   - Graduating college
   - Moving
   - Losing a loved one
   - Retiring

```
     ⌒⌒⌒⌒⌒⌒⌒⌒⌒⌒⌒⌒⌒⌒⌒⌒⌒
   ( All New Beginnings Start with an End )
     ⌣⌣⌣⌣⌣⌣⌣⌣⌣⌣⌣⌣⌣⌣⌣⌣⌣

        ╭─────────╮
       │    End    │
       │ Graduating│
       │  Moving   │
       │Losing Loved One│
       │  Retiring │
        ╰─────────╯

   ━━━━▶
```

This phase is when we identify what we are losing and learn how to manage those losses. It is recognizing what is truly over and being left behind, as well as what we can keep and incorporate into our new identity. In retirement terms, it's *letting go.* And while these events are endings, they all force one right into the next phase.

2. *The second phase is the neutral zone.* It's the in-between time when the old is gone but the new isn't here yet. It's the time between our past identity and our new one. If it was a job we lost, this phase would be the job search. If it was a lost loved one, it includes the stages of grief, and then the search for "What am I going to do now?" This phase can be short or long. It's the time between an end and a new beginning. A door has closed…and a window has not opened quite yet.

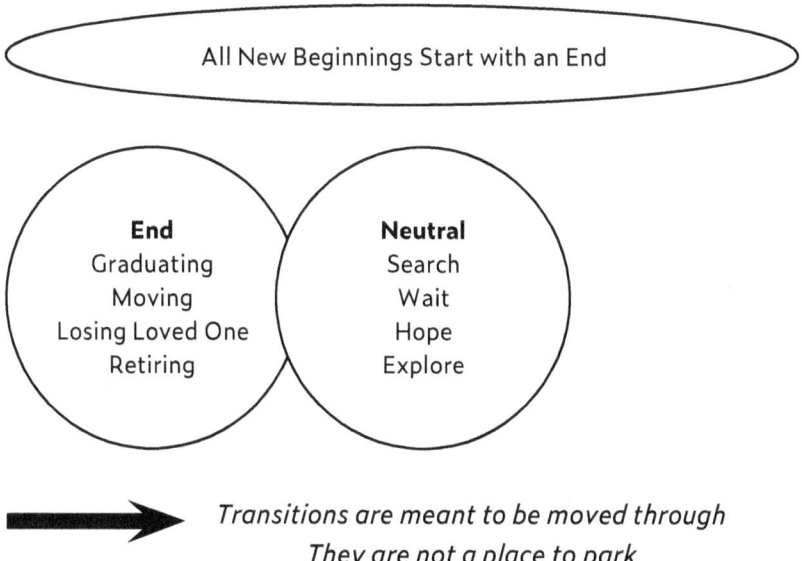

*Transitions are meant to be moved through
They are not a place to park*

In retirement terms: It's the search for what you will retire *to*. We explore, try new things, and go searching in a variety of directions. It's important to note it's easy to get stuck in this phase—too easy, in fact. When you're in this "experimental phase," you are bouncing around trying things out and don't have to commit to any one direction yet. It might be a rough time for you, or you might be having fun with the variety. But the most you'll get from this stage is fun and pleasure. Your purpose and fulfillment are yet to come.

> During this phase, you'll ask yourself these questions over and over again: "What do I see myself doing? What do I want to do?" Don't be surprised if day after day, you answer with, "I don't know!"

This phase often requires someone else's help to pull you out of phase two and push you into phase three.

It's worth noting:

- *Transitions are meant to be moved through.*
- *They are not a place to park and stay.*

3. **Phase three is a fresh start.** We're filled with excitement, passion, and optimism. The birds are chirping, and Julie Andrews comes running over the hillside singing "The Hills are Alive!" There's music in the air, and you have a lighter step. Everything is more colorful, more vibrant. Life is good!

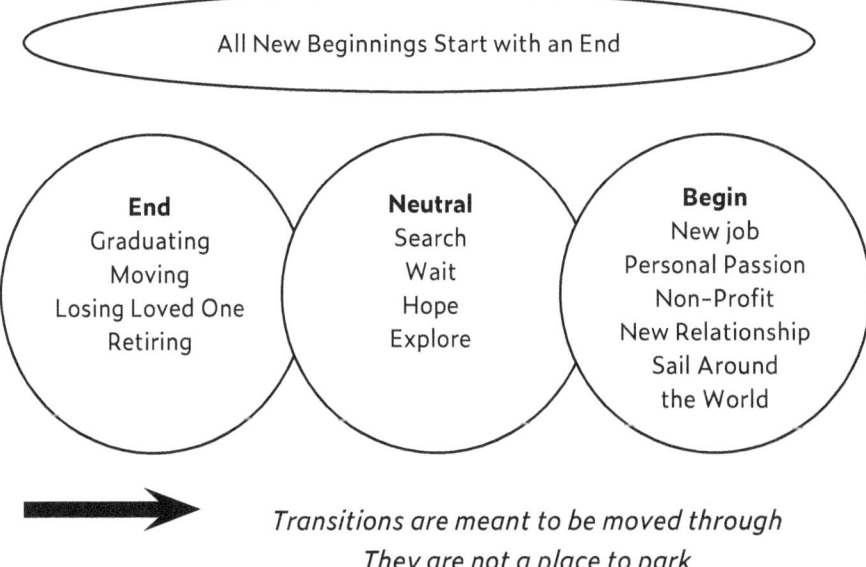

*Transitions are meant to be moved through
They are not a place to park*

In retirement terms, it's a new beginning. It could be a new job, discovering your personal passion, joining the board of a nonprofit, getting into or out of a relationship, or leaving to go sail around the world. You might be a new entrepreneur, tutor, or volunteer, or someone who could fundraise for a good cause. Hopefully, it's something that gives you purpose and fulfillment. And ultimately, you'll have the feeling you are part of something larger than yourself. You will have found new ways of being:

- Needed
- Involved
- Respected
- Valued

You will feel alive again; you'll have *purpose and fulfillment.*

Take your time through the stages of transition, noting where you are in the process, and trust you will find your New Beginning.

Well done, and congratulations! You are now ready to play your encore. May your life in retirement be filled with passion, purpose, fun, and fulfillment.

Wishing you all the best on your encore journey.

Larry Jacobson
Chief Retirement Coach
Buoy Coaching

Contact: www.larryjacobson.com/contact

AFTERWORD

I was early in the field of nonfinancial retirement coaching. I had plenty of naysayers in the early years, but I knew I was onto something. I started coaching people on their encore after friends asked me how I did it. How did I go from CEO to sailor without even looking back? I realized because of my experience, I could really help those who needed more direction. So I took a year to reverse engineer my own journey, chronicling the thoughts, actions, frustrations, and hopes I had after my twenty-year corporate life came to an end. I put it all back together and the result was a professional-grade online video course, *Sail Into Retirement*, designed with just the nonfinancial aspect of retirement as its focus. You can find it at www.BuoyTraining.com.

To make that course information available to more people, I wrote this book for you, and I sincerely hope you enjoyed and learned from it.

Like many authors, I love connecting with my readers. I would love to hear about your Encore experience. Are you in the process of creating your ideal retirement to realize your dreams, or are you already basking in your success of moving on in your life? I truly want to help you on your journey, so please reach out if you need help. To that end, I'll be glad to spend half an hour with you on phone or Zoom, and I can often determine how to approach navigating your encore right during our first call.

You might need someone to hold you accountable, or perhaps you would benefit from someone cheering you on and encouraging you to take action? I'm happy to discuss your journey to your dream goal and the fears, hesitations, and hopes that go with it. Contact Larry Jacobson here: www.larryjacobson.com/contact.

On my website at www.LarryJacobson.com/author, you'll find nearly a hundred color photos from my sailing trip around the world and a thirty-minute video about the trip, as well as a link to purchase *The Boy Behind the Gate* in hard-bound, soft-bound, Audible, or Kindle editions.

I welcome all reader feedback, and I'd love to hear from you. And may I ask a favor please? Authors live and breathe and hopefully don't die on reviews. If you like this book, I would be most appreciative if you would post a positive review on Amazon. Positive reviews make all the difference.

Thanks for reading, and I wish you all the best finding your encore.

With respect,
—Larry Jacobson

ACKNOWLEDGEMENTS

My reinvention of myself all started when two CEOs started asking me questions about how I was able to transition from CEO to sailor. They became coaching clients, and their feedback and encouragement gave me the idea I was onto something. More coaching clients followed, and their appreciation of my work confirmed there was a need for nonfinancial retirement coaching. Every client who told me I helped them confirmed the viability of my chosen path. To all of these people, I say a heartfelt "Thank you."

Estimates are that every day in the United States, ten thousand people reach the age of sixty-five, and many of those retire that same day or close to it. You may be one of them, and to you who are reading this book, I say "Thank you," because you are my clients too. I'm confident that my system has helped you answer some of your questions and put you on a path to a great encore.

Here's to all of you and your "Encore! Encore! Encore!"
—Larry Jacobson

ABOUT THE AUTHOR

"Retirement is not the end, but rather the opportunity for a new beginning," says Larry Jacobson, a leading authority on non-fiscal retirement lifestyle planning. Jacobson's successful experience of making the shift from his own business career, retiring from the corporate world, and achieving his personal dreams is his proven model for coaching. His experience has attracted clients from all walks of life, including entrepreneurs, CEOs, doctors, attorneys, teachers, and public figures.

Jacobson believes everybody has an Encore in them after they retire from their career. "You get a do-over, how cool is that?" asks Larry. He coaches clients to discover their passions, and then helps them combine their passion, knowledge, and experience to build a *plan of action* for a retirement of fulfillment and purpose. "And don't forget about fun," he adds. Jacobson is also known for his leadership and entrepreneurship coaching and is a certified World Class Speaking Coach.

Successfully transitioning from CEO to sailor, Jacobson achieved his lifelong dream of sailing around the world. After that accomplishment, he went on to become an award-winning author and TEDx motivational speaker. Now, Buoy Coaching & Training focuses on helping clients redefine retirement. The groundbreaking Sail Into Retirement™ program has quickly achieved notoriety in the field. Now that same information is available to everyone in this book.

Larry was recently awarded the coveted Retirement Catalyst Award by the Retirement Coaches Association, "for opening new doors, creating new boundaries, influencing others, and being a major contributor to the field of Retirement Lifestyle Coaching."

A California native, circumnavigator, and adventurer, Jacobson has over fifty thousand blue water miles under his keel. Larry lives in the San Francisco Bay Area and welcomes new friends and inquiries: larryjacobson.com/contact